ABUNDANT PROGRESS

Maximising the gradual steps of the journey

ESTHER JACOB

ABUNDANT PROGRESS
Maximising the gradual steps of the journey

Copyright © 2022 by Esther Jacob

All rights reserved. No portion of this book without permission may be reproduced, stored in a retrieval system, or transmitted in any form – scanned, electronic, photocopied or recorded without written consent of the author as it is strictly prohibited. Excerpts and links may be used, provided that full and clear credit is given to the author with specific direction and reference to the original content.

If you would like to use material from the book for short quotations or occasional page copying for personal or group study, this is permitted other than for review purposes. However, prior written permission must be obtained on request by emailing the author on info@authenticworth.com.

Unless otherwise indicated, Scripture quotations are taken from the New International Version (NIV), the Amplified Version (AMP), the New Kings James Version (NKJV) and the Easy Standard Version (ESV).

Paperback ISBN: 978-1-7398998-1-3
Hardback ISBN: 978-1-7398998-2-0
eBook ISBN: 978-1-7398998-3-7

Published by: Authentic Worth
Website: www.authenticworth.com

Authentic Worth is bringing worth back into you through storytelling and book writing!

Abundant Progress

ACKNOWLEDGEMENTS

It's with great honour to give thanks to God who has entrusted me to write and publish my sixth book. The journey of writing takes focus and vision; for this reason, I want to thank my family, close friends, loved ones, sisters, brothers and everyone that's supported the vision of the writing journey; those far and near that continue to support Authentic Worth Publishing, it is highly appreciated. Thank you all very much!

Abundant Progress

PRAISE TESTIMONIALS FOR AUTHENTIC WORTH

Esther has done extremely well in writing many books, including her latest book, Confident Face. She has come very far in being an Author. May you continue to write and create more books and have many more events. I love attending Authentic Worth's events because they are very encouraging. I also love the way Esther expands on her events as she always explains the full meaning about her books' purpose and why she chose to write that specific book. As you read Esther's books, you take away a lot and learn from them all. I feel very encouraged in reading Esther's books, especially the first book called *It's Time to Heal,* alongside Completion, From Glory to Glory and Confident Face which are my top four favourite books; they have really encouraged me in different aspects. I will definitely be purchasing more books when they come out and will support Authentic Worth – **Maria Agbarha.**

Authentic Worth led by Esther Jacob is a hub of great information. Starting out as an indie book author, I needed all the information I could find. I remember attending several of the Authentic Worth's in-person and online events and found each session insightful and inspiring! I also had a few accountability sessions with Esther earlier on and found her to be forthcoming with information, encouraging and ready to answer any questions I might have – **Anu Adebogun.**

I want to thank Esther and the team at Authentic Worth Publishing for an amazing service. Esther has been my rock from day one! Constantly giving me encouragement and being my accountability partner. Her guidance and support have been absolutely first class. Her knowledge of publishing is absolutely incredible. I would not have been able to complete my book without her. I fully recommend for anyone who is thinking about writing a book to get in touch. She will hold your hand right through the journey – **Des Amey.**

I attended a publishing event by Authentic Worth and would like to express how much of a blessing it was. Esther is an inspiration to aspiring authors and her books have so much meaning. I enjoyed the

Abundant Progress

conversations at the end of the event which were very transparent and encouraging. Will definitely be attending more events! – **Nkechi Ugbade.**

I attended an event organised by Authentic Worth Publishing, and as always, it was very informative, engaging and fun at the same time. It was a great opportunity to learn about the business, network and socialise with some wonderful people. I look forward to future events and the awesome things that are yet to be accomplished through this wonderful organisation. Thank you and keep up the great work! You're impacting lives! – **Charlotte Ajani.**

My 1-2-1 consultation with Esther was brilliant. Esther was very professional. I came away feeling inspired and encouraged with more clarity on the publishing process and with a clearer vision for my book. I look forward to working with Authentic Worth and highly recommend Esther – **Latoya Labor.**

Thanks for inviting me to the Authors of our Generation event Esther. I enjoyed the relaxed and interactive event. I liked hearing the writer's journeys and why they decided to write their books. The main take away for me was the value of sharing, and just because someone else has written on the topic before doesn't mean your story is not relevant. – **Charmaine Dawkins-Alder.**

I attended Authentic Worth's workshop on building self-confidence and personal development. It was absolutely everything I needed! The guest speakers were amazing. Esther was amazing and every event Authentic Worth puts on is always worth attending. I'm never empty by the end of it! Looking forward to making some positive life changes. I'm fuelled and inspired! Thank you for everything you do Esther! – **Jesse Konadu.**

Abundant Progress

TO THE READER OF ABUNDANT PROGRESS

Progress is gradual. Abundance is vast. Put them together and it will take you on a journey. Be proud of how far you've come and expectant for greatness ahead. Cherish the lessons learnt from the past and walk in boldness. Don't look at what you don't yet have, but believe that what you desire is already in front of you.

Go and achieve that abundant life because it is already in you, although it may take some time, it doesn't mean that you won't get there. Slow down and let life flow organically. Every moment in your life matters and is leading you towards the right path uniquely created for you. There is no need to look at what others are doing because your path and their path aren't the same. Confidence is already embedded in you and being able to ask for help is a sign of strength.

You can live your best life when you understand that abundance is in stages. It's in the giving, the sacrifice of time for family, loved ones, friends and the connections built within the community. It is being able to take the experiences that life has shown you to become better, being able to untie yourself from anything or anyone that is hindering your progress, but ultimately, remember this – you are capable of hindering your own progress without realising it.

Live with purpose and good intentions, not having thoughts only of yourself, but being able to think about other people too. What good is it to only have a life full of self? Don't the pagans do that? Abundance awaits you! Your peace, joy and happiness are in front of you, but when the opportunities come knocking at your door, will you be the one to open it, or will you let it pass you by? Will you be able to control the thoughts that go through your mind, making you focus on what you once had?

Don't resist change because it's important to your personal development. Change of seasons, friendships and environments are

Abundant Progress

all crucial to your personal and professional growth. Being open to meeting new people, exploring different cultures and making new friends with others yields signs of growth to learn about additional strengths you wouldn't have known had you stayed in your comfort zone. There are many areas in your life that must be challenged before it can be rewarded. It is with humility that you aim higher than where you already are, whilst being able to handle constructive criticism.

You are fully capable of making it in life without no one hindering or keeping you back from your destiny. The moments where your thoughts ran 360 were the times where you had to find yourself, look within and answer those hard questions. Find time to cry and let out all the tension, anger and frustration because that's the starting point of the healing process. It's a way of saying that you are ready for the next level.

Abundant progress teaches you about the stages of beauty in the *process*, and not just arriving at the destination. Relax because your life is in the Capable Hands of the One who knows you intimately. Everyone will go through different seasons of change, but that's where true transformation begins and the willingness to let go of what you had in mind to ultimately enjoy your unique journey to abundant progress.

Patience is a pivotal part of the process because it disciplines your mind for what you believe you are ready for, whilst testing times indicate what you know in order to effectively reach the next phase of your life. Abundance is achieved by adding value and multiplying your gifts in the lives of others.

Ultimately, we learn to build inner confidence of character by maintaining a stable attitude of being reformed to better serve those around us, therefore leading to progression in every area of our lives and lacking nothing. So, let's enjoy the journey of living an abundant life!

Abundant Progress

INTRODUCTION

Abundance - wealth, riches, peace, influence, power, legacy, strength, positivity! I am not the woman who fulfils multiple tasks at once within a short timeframe because I know what I can handle. I know how detrimental that can be to the mind due to the society and world we live in today. If you don't show how many accolades you've achieved or post them on social media, clearly, something is wrong. Not the case.

You must understand that in this life, if you allow circumstances and your environments to shape you to become what they want you to be, you won't have any desire of your own and make decisions suitable to you and your well-being.

Burnout is not good at all. You don't ever want to get to a stage in your life where you've toiled, struggled and worked countless of hours to reap little back. You don't just make it in one day. You work at it with all your heart with a spirit of excellence.

This is why I stand on committing every plan, every desire and every request into the Hands of God, for He knows your life from start to finish. Matthew 6:33 sums up the title of this book; abundant progress – the progress and steps we ought to take to be confident that as we seek God first, not second, He will show us the way to go, and all the other desires will follow. Our lives become intoxicated with what we see, what we *should* be doing at a certain age, or why we aren't where we believe we ought to be.

When I hear people talk about their lives, or how much they feel left behind, it makes us realise that we don't own time. Do not get me wrong, I strongly believe that there are great blessings that we should have at an appointed time and shouldn't be delayed at all. However, it depends on the way you live your life in obedience, thanksgiving and the willingness in allowing God to have His way.

Abundant Progress

When you sow well, you are able to reap well. Do not underestimate your progress because eventually, it will end up being abundant.
In order to get to the *abundance stage*, we must be humble and willing to start with what we have. If you constantly keep complaining about your life and where you are right now, it could be the barrier that's preventing you from seeing the beauty of life's progress.

Question: What did you rush in the past that ended up not working out the way you expected it to? At some point, we have all been in that desperate season of wanting every plan to be executed according to our schedule. I am aware. We live in an instant-gratified world where everything is NOW, NOW, NOW and when you get your desires, you complain that it is difficult to manage, but you forgot to appreciate that *hard times build you*. Why are you rushing my dear sister? Why are you anxious my brother?

I am not saying that you must remain stagnant and expect everything to come your way without working hard, no. There are people who choose not to work, so they are in a different category, but for those who are capable and able to work and function, what are you doing with your life? We can become so restless and concerned about life. We are only in today and we think about what will happen in the next two months or two years!

Don't worry about tomorrow, because every day has its own unique troubles. We should honour our own journey and where we are, not being intimidated by other people's progress. Those around us should encourage our personal walk to improvement and developing closeness with God.

Your imaginations can take you so far, but greater is revealed to those who learn to trust the process and believe more is to come. Don't settle. Know your value and what you bring to the table. We all desire to have abundance in all areas of our lives, so why not start today? Get ready to abundantly progress into the best version of yourself!

CHAPTERS

ONE   1
SLOW GROWTH

TWO   15
CLOUDED VISION

THREE   27
THE COMPARISON TRAP

FOUR   42
UNEXPECTED BREAKTHROUGH

FIVE   54
THE ART OF GRATITUDE

SIX   67
'ABUNDANCE' AND 'PROGRESS'

SEVEN   76
YOUR FAITH MATTERS

EIGHT   89
EXCELLENCE TO EXCELLENT

REFLECTION   103

Abundant Progress

ONE

SLOW GROWTH

"Go slower!"
"You are moving too fast!"
"Don't rush!"
"Who are you trying to impress?"
"Look at your age mates! They have achieved so much more!"

Have you heard these words before? Whether you've heard them from family or friends, there is a stigma of fear, abandonment, tension and denial. It's becoming more frequent in our instant-gratified society. We want to look the part, so we take shortcuts in the hopes of getting to our desired destination, only to realise that we have to re-take the test again. No matter what your life looks like right now, all the decisions, hard work, and resilience you are putting into each day is building up a great legacy for future generations whilst building your tenacity and character.

I remember a time where life felt extremely slow for me – eager to see great results in my business and positive changes in my skincare routine in such a short space of time. I had to be realistic about the growth I'd desired to see and embrace the slow seasons. To tell you that growing slowly can be painful, there will always be those who you know that are doing better, but when it comes to you, all you can see is blur. Why is it easy to focus on what others are doing and become accustomed to judging your life based on someone else's lifestyle?

The process of slow growth can be seen from different perspectives in either good, mutual or painful ways of living. Has it occurred to you that as you go higher in life, it starts to gradually become lonely? The pain of thinking you are left behind does more damage than you'd think.

Abundant Progress

I believe it's important not to force anything to happen in life. When you do this, you become tensed and start working in your own strength. There are days where it seems out of control and all you want to do is give up, but in those moments, it teaches us to pause and see our lives from another angle; what is the process of giving up teaching me? Rather than throwing in the towel, we must come face-to-face with those hard times, being honest about our growth and develop a patient spirit in the process.

Pain is where your assignment is – this is the classroom where you have to embrace and learn how to welcome pain.

What triggers you the most is not only your pain point, but what God is using to change your heart. As hard as it is to accept pain, it is teaching you how to be strong and handle it with maturity. Whether it's dealing with the pressure of settling down, getting married, having children, and so many other pressures that society portrays. How many of us can relate to those moments where we hear the voices of 'So, how is life going for you? Are you dating or seeing anyone?' – Yes! The questions will come. It happens. I believe that the trend to settle for fear of being 'left behind' is what causes women and men to miss out on God's best because their slow season begins to become a heavy burden, rather, it is God preparing them for the greatest blessing they've been waiting for and enjoying it too.

The ability to act perfect in an imperfect world causes many pressures. Oh, when will the pressure of life stop? To every reader; remember that you only have one life which is precious. The responsibility for people to believe in you before you believe in yourself has to stop. Nobody should be at the mercy of anyone else other than the God that created you in His own image. Waking up each day to expect greatness and for it to turn back into frustration and delay makes you question the essence of life. The pace of life causes many of us, if not all, at times to rush for what we haven't been trained to accomplish. The lessons you learn along the way are here to teach you about yourself and building up character, patience, integrity and the ability to keep believing for a better tomorrow.

Abundant Progress

What are some of the reasons we might be experiencing slow growth? Let's take a look at the following:

- **Ingratitude** – when life becomes busy and booked, it is easy to become overwhelmed with many activities and forget the One who granted you access to the opportunities in the first place. Life is always on the go, but have you taken a moment to be thankful for how far you've come, or is there always something to complain about causing slower growth in your life to occur? The more you complain, the longer you will stay in that position you're in.

- **Stagnation** – if there's anything life keeps teaching me is not to stay in one place. Stagnation causes comfortability and a lazy mindset. The longer you are in the wilderness without learning from your season, the longer your waiting period. In other words, there is something that stagnation teaches you in the wilderness that leads you into greatness. Don't you know that for every dry season, there must be a time limit and the abundance of rain will come? You can't stay stagnant forever and think it is normal. No – learn to keep moving for the benefit of future generations. Staying in one position and not training upcoming leaders causes conflict and is one of the main reasons most authorities stay in power but lack vision and wisdom in dealing with current affairs and future delegations.

- **Lack of prayer life and communication with God** – your prayer life matters! Do not be concerned or surprised when trials come and you haven't taken the time to seek God. Communication is also a key attitude to progress. Entertaining slow growth is when you've stop talking and kept your mouth closed. A closed mouth is a closed destiny. This is not the life God wants you to have. Of course, there is a time and season for everything under the sun, but when you find yourself in a situation that seems impossible to come out of, you must learn how to consecrate yourself and spend quality time in prayer. Remember that your tears are

Abundant Progress

also expressions of communication, especially when you don't have the words to say.

- **Being out of alignment** – Not being in alignment is dangerous. You can be easily swayed by what you see, hear or feel. Being out of alignment is costly to your destiny as you may end up listening to everyone else but your own heart. When was the last time you made a decision that suited you best? Or do you feel most comfortable agreeing with what looks like the best route that you've forgotten the power of your own decisions?

- **Character development** – Before the contract or collaborative opportunity comes your way and you decide to sign it, or the man that shows interest decides to ask you out for dinner, be reminded that character attracts people to you. If your character does not live up to who you are, it will cause confusion towards the other party. Character development is pivotal in any stage of life you are in. Don't let social media make you change for instant gratification. Life teaches you how to conduct yourself as your character will change due to circumstances, however, it is meant to help you become better.

- **Your environment** – The people you associate yourself with are a reflection of you. Be aware of the people you entertain as you continue going higher. Slow growth is caused by the people you surround yourself with, particularly those that subtract from you and don't add value. You need *value-added* friends in every season you encounter. Some people will be in your life for a season, a reason or a lifetime. Regardless of how long people stay in your life, they are there to teach you key lessons and you have to learn how to let people go when they have contributed their part.

- **Not acknowledging your wrongdoings** – No matter what you have done, being able to identify where you have gone wrong and seek God to ask for His forgiveness is vital to see change in your life. Living in guilt and assuming that you

Abundant Progress

aren't forgiven is what causes so much dysfunction, making you question who you are and ultimately doubting God's promises over you. Before you ask for anything, it is important to be real with God to reveal where you've messed up, and accept His tender loving forgiveness. Through confessions of wrong doing, the healing begins.

When someone says 'you are moving too fast,' how do you respond? To an extent, you can take it from two perspectives. The **first** scenario could be a family friend or relative encouraging you to do thorough research before stepping into business, or the relationship you desire to be in so much. The **second** scenario could be where you end up making quick decisions that impact future destinies and generations to come, for example; buying now and paying later or not investing in future endeavours to improve financial literacy. You constantly keep certain visions in your mind and assuming they won't work, you end up not trying at all. This causes so much delay, not only to others but to your own life too. In every season, there is a time to move and a time to be still. Only you will know the type of season you are in which will determine the moves you make; however, those moves must be handled with **wisdom** and **effective strategy**.

What key decisions are you looking to make right now to avoid slow growth taking over your life? Write them down here:

_____

_____

_____

_____

_____

_____

Abundant Progress

Slow growth isn't always comfortable, but it does have great benefits. I remember a time speaking to a friend about the beauty of being prepared for what we desire. We want the glamourous blessings, but easily forget that they take a lot of time, focus, patience and daily preparation, whether that's being more financially stable and knowing how to manage money, to buying a property for the first time.

Reading *Abundant Progress* will make you come across a moment in your life where you ask when you'll become a home owner. The questions to consider when preparing is: "How are you managing where you currently live?" and "What contributions are you making around the house?" These are to be pondered on before considering to be positioned as an owner of your home in due course.

How you treat your current home is how you will treat your future home.

We have to be mindful of how we manage the little tasks before asking for greater abundance. Dreaming big is great, but do you have the mental and emotional capacity to handle what you are asking for? There is a tendency to look the part, but not having what you desire is painful. Living a life that is way beyond your financial means is not wisdom at all. Being envious or jealous of someone that has made it to the next level won't make your blessings come any quicker. You must understand that slow growth is working for your good. Every day when we wake up is an opportunity to look ahead to the future with great joy and expectation, however, starting with one day at a time.

When you end up worrying about what hasn't yet happened, it will rob you of the present moment. To you, life may seem slow, but to the One that knows everything about you, He sees the end from the beginning. The beauty about slow growth is that it causes you to stay focused on the present moment. There is nothing you can do to speed up the process, unless you take shortcuts and end up starting over. The hunger to look successful but the impatience to wait and

Abundant Progress

improve our lives each day are constantly in battle, let alone waiting for something that feels like a lifetime causes people to become dysfunctional. When Hannah in the Bible waited to have a child, Peninnah kept manipulating her. For further study, read 1 Samuel 1:1-20.

It felt like nothing was happening, but the courage Hannah took to keep fighting through prayer and weeping will forever inspire me. It helps me to know that in life, no matter who does or doesn't believe in you, when you want an abundant life, you have to go through the steps of progression. It was difficult for Hannah seeing her rival Peninnah having babies, and thought there was something wrong with her. She could not understand why God was taking so long to grant her earnest desire. Imagine being so distressed to the extent that you stop believing. It hurts! Yes, it does. However, it's in those vulnerable seasons that you make an intentional decision to get up and turn your life around.

It's easy to speak defeating words when all you see is slow growth, but remember to encourage yourself that a day will come when the fear will eventually subside, causing you to rejoice that you waited. A favourite song of mine called *You Waited* by Travis Greene continues to humble me as it expresses that God waited patiently to give me His best. When the time comes for you to think and dwell on the days, months or years you've waited for something great to happen, and tears start streaming down your face, you will appreciate when the blessings come unexpectantly. If we could adapt the mindset of embracing delayed gratification and remember how good it is for us, we will see life from a different perspective.

Abundance is costly and you must have the character to maintain its position.

What one may consider as slow growth could be considered quick transformation to another individual. I've had moments in my life where it felt like certain requests seemed quite slow and couldn't always understand why they were taking long. A quote that goes around often on social media says: "You aren't waiting for God;

Abundant Progress

God is waiting for you" – which is such a profound statement, but what about when you are convinced that you've given God your best and yet, it still feels slow? What if you are putting in all the hard work, effort, time and late nights and still don't see the fruit of your labour? I believe a lot of us have and at times, continue to experience this. The word I want to give you is; be **consistent**. It may hurt for a while because all you are doing may not fall in alignment, but it will surely come to fruition at the appointed time.

The importance of having a great environment of people cheering you on is also a positive contributing factor to seeing progress happen. We don't want to end up pretending that we are happy when deep down, we are still counting the years gone and nothing 'seems' to be happening. I laugh now because those days are over! The moments where God kept me waiting for certain manifestations was the beauty of His greatness working when He saw I was ready. A great blessing that's given too soon isn't a blessing at all and will take time to nurture, develop and ultimately bring internal and external transformation.

Let's talk about something you are passionate about. This could be your job, being in a relationship that leads to marriage, investments and finances, being a positive mental health advocate, etc. All these passions take time to develop. The generation we are in constantly causes you to look at yourself and label the resources you don't yet have and cause you to be discontent.

⇒ Slow growth is present to keep you humble and avoid boasting.
⇒ Slow growth is present to remind you that doing anything without God's guidance will lead to vain outcomes.

We must remember that our time in life matters and how we live reflects on future generations. Yes, it is frustrating to wait, but it's working well for your character development and growth, causing you not to depend on others. Our expectations aren't in the hands of anyone, especially in the world we're in that constantly changes on

Abundant Progress

what's hot and what's not. We should endeavour to maintain the practical insights into slow growth allowing it to work for our good.

Slow growth isn't a bad thing; it's the way you perceive it to be that becomes the problem. What lens are you looking at yourself from, and what limiting thoughts have made you think like a survivor and not a successor? Your mind can either work for or against you, but the responsibility is in your hands. It's easy to think that life isn't on your side because of all the past mistakes that's been made, however, for every decision, they've shaped the individual you are today.

It's not about being comfortable and making life fit the way you desire; there will be temptations to shortcut the journey, but when you come out on the other side, you notice certain cracks that haven't been mended because of instant gratification and the ignorance of not checking the root of the matter which is the unwillingness to let go of your pain.

You can look good by adorning yourself, but lacking good manners and character-flaws doesn't produce growth. To look at yourself in the mirror and know where you stand is important, and being able to write down all the areas in your life that you feel is slowing you down is also therapeutic to your well-being. No matter who you are, flaws are everywhere, and that's what makes you unique.

We aren't made to be perfect, but we are made to progress.

The greatest decision especially in a season of stillness is to seek God first. I like to encourage my friends about speaking to the One that knows everything. Secondly, to pray over what is disturbing your peace and trust the lessons they're teaching you. Slow growth isn't always bad; it gives you balance and the willingness to help others in their seasons of waiting. You are more likely to be trusted in the process of waiting because people will see that you've been able to endure trials. This is why those who wait the longest will be blessed the greatest. There's something about seeing other people moving ahead, whilst it seems like you are still in the same position

Abundant Progress

for years, UNTIL GOD steps in and shows you why He had you in the waiting room.

For others, they become weary in the waiting season because their minds haven't been trained to be patient. On the other hand, others have been trained to endure the waiting seasons and fill it with positive joy, hope and expectation and ultimately, being able to serve one another. I remember in 2018, a friend said to me; 'Esther, if you desire to get married, serve a married couple.' This spoke to me as I understood the importance of being a blessing onto those that have what I desire.

In your season of steady growth, learn how to serve someone else no matter who they are. You don't know who has the key to the next dimension of your life. We don't have to wait until someone makes it to the top to serve them, but we can help them when they don't believe in themselves. It's these small yet powerful alterations to life that causes gradual change.

Change can't always be seen, and you probably won't notice them when they arrive, but you know when freedom hits your heart when what used to bother you has no power anymore. You can have limited funds but utilise the gift of speaking, singing or dancing to keep your mind away from temptation and complacency.

Society constantly waits for their best life to appear when they are forgetting that their best life starts right now, not when life is good to them. Life is always good when you ponder on the goodness of God and the rich gift of being alive and well. Life isn't good for those who manipulate or use others to get to the top leaving them behind.

When you are in the season of slow growth, don't use people to get to the top. Help them even when you are struggling, for two heads are better than one. It's more effective when you plan strategically and work with others who are on a similar journey with you where both parties can share ideas. As stated before, the slow growth season can take a lot out of you. It doesn't mean you are doing

Abundant Progress

something wrong. You can be honest with where you are right now and control your emotions.

Doing everything on your own will cause unnecessary burnout that doesn't allow you to be your authentic self. You may have to wait for years until you see the breakthrough come, but it doesn't change who you are or who God is. The pressure to perform and be in certain situations that cause you to become fearful contributes to the slow season. The world will look down on you because you haven't achieved the level they are on, but if you don't come to the realisation that perfectionism doesn't exist, but progress is paramount, you will always end up battling and competing with results that never existed in the first place.

Placing emphasis and being too hard on yourself doesn't amount to healthy well-being. Forcing your way to connect with others without genuinely developing an organic and authentic relationship isn't going to win you the deal. True intentions always show in seasons of pressure and uncertainty. Can you weigh out a season in your life where it became difficult to handle? You've heard the bad news and now you have to start again; how do you cope with that?

Can you handle not knowing what the next season will look like? It's not always easy because our itching ears are eager to know what life will look like on the other side. When you reach a certain milestone, there is still so much to learn, and life is beautiful because it enables you to go through the process of acquiring wisdom and applying it in tough slow seasons.

The moments of slow growth aren't permanent, but are present to keep you moving ahead. For it is better to fight stagnation than opposition because you are your greatest encourager. To be stagnant is to be uncomfortable, and when you feel as if nothing is happening in your life, this isn't a matter of other people contributing positively or negatively; this is more to do with how YOU see your own progress and work on the areas that are flat or inactive. When your plans aren't working, it's easy to forfeit them and try another way or strategy. No matter how many times you do something different,

Abundant Progress

it is not advisable to switch immediately when it doesn't work. You have to give it time to evolve, develop and enhance.

Building a business is about developing your character which is ongoing. Don't underestimate the slow progress in your life because you want quick results. Having the wrong character and abundant wealth will cause dysfunction which eventually leads to lost opportunities and misplaced networks.

Your environment is watching and how you live is a reflection of how they will see you. Be gentle and patient with your journey and never look down on the slow process. What you can't see right now is not the problem; it's the mentality to work with what you already have to make your goals achievable. You may never realise the power of what's in your hand until it's in the Hands of God. When we submit our burdens to Him, our slow growth gradually improves as time goes by. We may not see this growth instantly, but it is always working for our utmost good.

It's also good to speak about your life, your journey and where you currently are. Communication is a powerful tool in expressing yourself and being able to mentally position yourself for change. The mind is YOUR greatest asset that keeps you going and remain accountable to your personal growth. Although we are exposed to many distractions, we possess the gift of **self-control** that reminds us of what to feed and what to starve.

I want to emphasise on the importance of being slow; our generation sees slowness as a bad thing, particularly when it comes to age, occupation, how much money is in the bank, relationship status, business growth; to name a few. Being defined or allowing society to make you second guess yourself because of where you currently are doesn't allow God to fill your heart with peace of mind.

It makes you easily vulnerable to what you see rather than walking in the belief that He already has you. Eventually, you start to work and think in your own strength, becoming your own hero to then eventually stumble and remember that all this while, His Presence constantly follows you. The beauty of being patient when life

Abundant Progress

becomes slow is when you are able to learn more effectively than having everything go the way you intended it to.

Even when plans don't go the way you expected it to be, it is still beautiful. Isaiah 55:8 reminds us that God's ways and our ways are different, and when He disciplines us, He wants us to abide and obey, not quarrel or complain. Slow growth is gradual and eventually, it stimulates positive mental, physical, psychological, and emotional healing to occur. What you used to wait years for has finally come at a time you least expected it, because God knew you were ready to handle it. A good father will wait patiently at the appointed time to give their children blessings they can enjoy.

The future generation that's coming after us will learn from what we are currently doing and for this reason, when we succumb to putting in little effort, we shouldn't expect a great result in the long-term if it hasn't been developed, grounded or tested. Every slow season in your life will be tested because without them, there will be no testimony. Endeavour to be open to change during slow seasons of growth and surround yourself with other people that are more knowledgeable and willing to help you move to the next level.

Slow growth reminds you that life isn't in your own pace, but gradually, you learn to embrace what each season teaches you. Your life is doing what it needs to do and your responsibility is turning every lesson into blessings and utilising every opportunity to grow within. Don't put pressure on yourself by becoming uneasy and worried that you are behind. Take the time to understand yourself and know your strengths and weaknesses; be content in the season you are in knowing that going backwards is not an option! Where you are now is preparing you for the journey ahead; you don't need to keep looking back and comparing the slow growth you're experiencing.

Be intentional and choose to be thankful for the lessons you've learnt during the slow stages of life. When someone comes into your life and shares their story with you about their journey, it will inspire you to keep on going. You may not fully know what someone else is going through as it doesn't make anyone exempt from seasons of

Abundant Progress

slow movement. At times, it's the lessons that are revealed in dark moments that cause you to appreciate the blessings that are in motion. To be able to handle what you are asking for is a blessing in itself, and as the saying goes: 'less is more' if it's in the right hands. Utilise what you have well because what's in you is greater than what you are looking elsewhere for.

Whether you realise it or not, God is always working in your life! The key is not to miss what He is doing because you feel uncomfortable in the current season. When the slow seasons come, it is an opportunity to draw you closer to His Presence and make Himself known to you. The slow moments made me realise how much love God had for me that He didn't want me to rush but embrace each step of the way. You are responsible for the thoughts you have – this includes how willing you are able to work effectively without trying to force situations when they aren't yet ready to blossom.

You are learning every day in different ways and the progress you are making is because you chose to take that road. Be wise and willing to let go of the stigma to have everything together. Be free to change and learn new skills that require you to grow internally first and eventually you'll start to blossom outwardly. You will look back and thank the slow growth that you didn't rush.

A reminder for you: Don't rush in life – remember that you are here for a purpose and the desires you're still waiting on aren't forgotten. Being in haste doesn't bring about the best results, so learn how to take your life each day at a time. Your determination to grow gracefully will allow others to perform well and naturally. A rushed seed that isn't nurtured with care can't produce its best fruit. Wait patiently because you will blossom at the appointed time!

TWO

CLOUDED VISION

That moment when you wake up from your nap, and all of a sudden, you feel overwhelmed with clouded vision. It could be a dream that made you think about your life or caused you not to take anything for granted. For those who understand the importance of having a positive and healthy mindset, you would know that thoughts eventually reveal itself through words. Wandering thoughts of becoming easily led by feelings entangled with past mistakes will make it difficult to overcome clouded vision. What you desire to achieve will take proactive steps, and this starts with removing all the obstacles that cause you to make quick decisions.

Think of it this way; when you want to plant a seed, you have to analyse the soil. The soil has to be clean and adaptable to the seed you are going to plant. In other words, let's get to the root of the matter – our lives will take different turns, from the way we respond to it to the results received in the years to come. However, I want to focus on analysing the 'heart' of the matter. The roots that are stemmed within us come from our thoughts.

The thoughts we accumulate start from the motives and intentions we have towards ourselves, and in turn, other people. No matter who you are or what position you are in, it is important to look at life from a healthy perspective. Waking up to complaints, groans, and confusion doesn't contribute to a healthy body.

Clouded vision is a responsibility that we must endeavour to take responsibility of. Being in a vulnerable situation without getting to the root of the matter won't solve the problem. You can be real with a trusted individual to speak about what is going on in your life. When anger is boiled up in your heart, how long will you allow it to aggravate you before it starts manifesting towards those around you?

Abundant Progress

Your perspective could be lying to you about your future; that is why you have to change your mindset and be open to the way God intends to move in your life.

Even though life has its moments where it is difficult to see your way clear, it's still important to refuse the lies that your emotions express because they are not facts. Changing your perspective is just what you need to be open to the path God has for you. When we think a certain way, that is what we get because it becomes what we are accustomed to. When you start believing that you deserve less, you will start attracting less and accept anything that comes your way without clarity. No one reading this book should ever feel unworthy of who they are or the abundance they are to receive. **Believe that you deserve good in life** and wait in expectation; work well to achieve the life that you desire.

Clouded vision takes many forms, particularly in the way one relates to each other. One great key aspect that life has taught me is that seasons change and so will you. Those around you will change and vice versa. This is inevitable because as you continue to grow and get better, certain environments can't come with you and will have to be removed. Staying in one place for a length of time can impact the way you progress. We have a tendency to want to stay comfortable because, of course, it feels good for a while, but eventually, something starts working in you to seek for more. This isn't selfish but purposeful because life is a journey.

Each day you have in life teaches you valuable lessons; at times, it may not even make sense because it looks cloudy. The path of life isn't a straightforward road; tears will occur and silent struggles will start becoming restless and the like. However, what clouded vision teaches you is to trust the Teacher when you can't see the answers. We are easily influenced to leave the current season we are in to jump into the next, whereas we haven't passed the first hurdle or understood the reason why we are in a certain situation. This happens a lot especially in the millennial generation which must be addressed with maturity and encourage the importance of gratitude and meditation.

Abundant Progress

When you dwell on what you don't yet have, it causes you to amplify the tension. The desires of your heart will come at the appointed time, but you must also realise that preparation is the key contributing factor to receiving it. When it comes, you have to be responsible for nurturing it. Doing what looks popular leads to being out of alignment. Our minds tend to go round in circles because we don't feel good enough until that business corporation accepts our application, or the house is finally sold and the title will change to homeowner to impress others we don't have a relationship with.

In as much as these great blessings are gifts from God, it shouldn't deter you from your ultimate purpose in life. If you desire to start a business, particularly if you aren't from a business background, it's natural to have concerns. Your vision to run a successful business is there, but how to get it off the ground is what makes you question if you are good enough or assessing whether the business idea will last. When the doubts come in, use it as an indication to push you beyond the thoughts. If you need to take time out of your day to reflect, rest and recuperate, do so.

There will be times where breaks are needed especially when it doesn't seem like anything is working. Going backwards with the aim to move ahead in your life can become very time-consuming. You aren't sure whether it will work out or not; no matter the season you are in, find courage to know that everything is working out for your good. Don't settle in those thoughts for too long. Yes, it is easier said than done, but as we grow older, we must also possess wisdom and knowledge. The setbacks of life should not impact the vision we have because when you are building a legacy or creating impact and freedom for the community, you will have seasons of rejection and double-minded thoughts.

In these situations, ask yourself what you are willing to learn from them. Rejection, on the other hand, is constantly working for your highest good, teaching you to wait for better to come. Sometimes, what we think is vision can be stemmed from environments that don't add value or cause you to question yourself. Your vision

Abundant Progress

should be smooth with the aim to inspire and ultimately bring change not only to your life, but in the lives of others.

Our lives are cycles. What we bring to the table is what we will also get back. No matter who you are, we all need one another. No one can manage life on their own. Your business may be successful, but remember that you had people in your life that believed in your vision and invested their time, money and effort in your idea. As they take the time to invest and work with you, it is important to reciprocate this back. Finances are one of the key contributing factors to business success, however, we must remember to build genuine relationships with others to gradually progress as we learn from those around us. The importance of building good connections and flourishing networks is stemmed from how we treat one another to see growth.

Having a vision that's going to impact generations will require sacrifice and effort on both ends. Never looking down on yourself is paramount to gaining and building key relationships. The relationships you have around you, however, can either amplify your vision or block it. Not everyone will agree with what you believe in, neither will everyone invest in your vision, but the most important aspect to remember is to keep feeding your relationships and be open for others to invest in you with words of encouragement and support. It doesn't matter how long you have known someone or not, there are lessons to learn from those you meet.

The power of listening to another person speak from their heart is honourable, respectful and humbling, especially when they don't feel their life is matching up to their expectations. There is only so much we can do to cover up and show our good sides without being honest and open-minded about the days we struggle with. Everyone to a certain extent struggles with a weakness and there is no shame in that.

The frustration we have today is when we live a life where we **pretend** to have it all together, when in reality, there are still moments in our lives where we feel incomplete and empty. This is normal, but it's not normal to pretend. You can speak out, you can

Abundant Progress

cry, you can vent and be honest with your season. It may be cloudy right now, but the sun will soon shine if you allow it to.

Fulfilment and being at ease is what we desire, however, when life comes with an unclear vision, anxiety gradually starts settling in. Some people are disciplined at managing their emotions; therefore, they refuse to entertain anxiety because they know it causes health issues; others don't realise the impact it has on the body at a later stage. Our bodies are trained to handle a certain amount of pressure, but putting your mind, heart, spirit and soul at risk because you want to know everything about life is costly, let alone knowing what tomorrow holds.

The beauty is in the gradual stages of life. There are moments in our lives where we are eager to know why certain decisions were made or why we had to go through certain experiences, however, we must come to the realisation that we don't always need to understand every detail. As individuals, we want to justify that our answers have been met and understood.

Think of it this way; the Global Coronavirus Pandemic caused uncertainty, fear, loss, grief and so much pain. It made the world to be at a stand-still and yet, we want to understand why it happened in such a short amount of time that not only impacted nations, but people's lives, families and homes. The New Year of 2020 – 1st January; the excitement started about the year of *vision and abundance*, and despite all that happened throughout that year, it will never be forgotten in history.

We can't ever control how life operates because we don't know what tomorrow will hold. In 1 Corinthians 6:20, Apostle Paul stated to the Corinthian church that they were bought with a special price. How much more us and how we treat our lives. When you are in seasons of doubt, don't reject it; be present with your emotions because it is a part of you, however, don't let your emotions control you to make wrong decisions. Our lives are not our own, neither the visions we have; they must all be in submission to God's Will rather than fitting God into what we want Him to be. It takes great practise, discipline and surrendering everything in order to see our way clear.

Abundant Progress

Once you have surrendered, learn to be patient with the process and leave the outcome to do what it needs to do, because change isn't always quick as we expect it to be; it can start with gradual steps that we cultivate on a daily basis by being disciplined enough to know what to focus on and what to disregard. Our days are being numbered and how we live today prepares us for tomorrow. As God wakes us up each day, it is important to remember that you aren't dependent on anyone to make decisions, but to the One who knows your steps and having the comfort to know your steps are being ordered.

Declare Psalm 52:8 over your life which says: *"But I am like an olive tree flourishing in the house of God; I trust in God's unfailing love for ever and ever."* You will always flourish when you are in the right environment. Being in God's Presence is one of the most fruitful places to be, especially when you declare that His love is what sustains you each time. When you experience His love, there is a strong peace that comes even when situations try to disturb you. This isn't about working in your own strength but communicating with God about where you are and being real with Him.

When Psalm 52:8 says "I am", it declares two key components:

(1) God is the *I am that I am*, and;
(2) God prophesying into your own life.

It is costly to wait for someone to speak words of life into you, so ensure that you create time each day and speak what you desire to see.

When you see many distractions and enticing words that cling to you, your stomach begins to turn and your mind envisions how it will fit with your long-terms goals, but remember that no matter what you build in your mind, it must be in accordance to what God wants first before it comes to fruition. It is important to understand that our goals aren't necessarily bad, but if they don't have a strong foundation, it will ultimately end up becoming a clouded vision.

Abundant Progress

A friend spoke to me about transitioning from her three-year role as she wanted to start working from home or somewhere that was closer for convenience. She answered her own question when she contributed that she doesn't want to apply for any type of job, but a role that she is capable of doing and that's in her interest. When it comes to making decisions that require change, it's important to ask yourself what the purpose of the move is. ***Over to you***: answer the following questions on *why* you need to see these visions happen:

Why do you want to leave the job you're currently doing right now and what do you visualise yourself doing next?

_____

_____

_____

_____

_____

_____

If you had the opportunity to make 6 or 7 figures per annum, how would you use or delegate the finances? Think intentionally about this question…

_____

_____

_____

_____

Abundant Progress

_____

_____

_____

_____

What do you believe your vision or purpose is?

_____

_____

_____

_____

_____

_____

_____

When you have multiple thoughts in your mind, how do you handle them? When your business idea or career path seems unclear, how do you cope? As I was on the journey of creating a name for Authentic Worth, I took the word 'worth' from my blog and combined it with the word 'authentic.' From that time on, I decided to use my two books; It's Time to Heal and Completion to prepare me by starting off with workshops on storytelling and book writing in 2018. Looking back at your past experiences will give you a glimpse of what the future entails as you go through each day to remind you of your purpose.

God may not always give you the go-ahead or specific directions on where you need to be. He will, however, reveal them to you in stages and that can take time if you aren't in alignment with His Will. It's easy to think your way is better, but we must understand that God doesn't confuse those who put their full trust in Him as He speaks organically in a way that is clear; that gentle and subtle voice.

Abundant Progress

Due to the on-going pressure of wanting more, having one business is not enough let alone working a 9-5 full-time job; in God's eyes, He says 'my grace is sufficient for you' – 2 Corinthians 12:9. When you read this aloud, it does something to you! Try it now; say out loud: **'GOD'S GRACE IS SUFFICIENT FOR ME!'**

This scripture has been a pillar of strength since taking the leap of faith on leaving a legacy for upcoming and future authors to write their stories and turn them into published books, and the strength to keep walking in obedience. I can't emphasise enough on the beauty of obedience as it reminds me that I am not in charge of my life, neither do I want to carry the weight of understanding everything that happens.

Deciding to make peace with the way life is going is one of the greatest gifts you can give yourself including surrendering your plans for His ultimate plan. Nonetheless, it can be painful when you can't see your way clear. You hear and receive words of encouragement about abundance, and when you check your bank account, it's not what you expected. In those seasons, God is drawing you closer to Himself because He refuses to allow you to be distracted by your desires. Through obedience, that is when God is able to restore all that was lost in reference to Joel 2:25-26 for further study.

You will hear many stories or testimonies of those who've taken great leaps of faith to work hard and not have a *Plan B*. No matter whether the opportunity you seek for is paid or unpaid, do it to the Glory of God. When you call on Him and seek His direction, the peace you receive is enough for you to take another look at what you have and make it work for your good. When you value what is in your hands, opportunities will find you as long as you work it well. The gifts that you have are not for everyone to approve of before you step into greatness. Your greatness is attached to God's power that is working on the inside of you.

Describe your most painful season where it felt like everything you were trying to build didn't seem to work. This could be starting a

Abundant Progress

new role and not understanding the tasks you were given or starting a business without any financial support. When it becomes unbearable, it might not look enough, but it *is* enough. It may seem like you need more resources, more time, more opportunities, more money, but I tell you; what is already in your reach can be maximised when using the right tools *#mindsetstretch*. When you are feeling helpless, study Psalm 121:1-8. When you are honest about where you are, He will come and meet you at your point of need because God always wants to bless the real you. The words you spoke to Him has already been heard, so take the time to build patience and wait for a response.

At the same time, remember that your relationship with God shouldn't be transactional. It's not based on what God can do before you make a move. When you submit all your plans to Him, He will direct your decisions which will start to fall in place accordingly. You won't need to look to the left or the right; you will hear a voice telling you; 'This is the way; walk in it' in reference to Isaiah 30:21. Your steps are constantly being ordered by the Lord even when your life feels blurry. The following questions open up the opportunity to focus on specific areas where you've encountered slow growth and the decisions you came up with to overcome those seasons. Fill them out below:

What was your most painful and slowest season and how did this have an impact on your vision?

_____

_____

_____

_____

_____

Abundant Progress

What solutions did you come up with when the feeling of slow growth impacted your mental and emotional well-being?

_____
_____
_____
_____
_____
_____
_____

Having answered the questions, you will eventually understand the season you are in and identify whether you need to slow down, accept where you are or work on becoming internally healthier. All these components lead to an abundant life through your mental and emotional wellness and stability. You don't need to be consumed about what others are doing, but to realise that the responsibility you have is to keep moving and work on areas that need improvement.

When you are constantly looking at your life from a doubtful perspective, you will continue to encourage more doubt your way. There are many opportunities around you each day and until you learn how to embrace them, you will continually miss them all. Don't let this be you!

The vision you have for your life can only come from a heart that is willing to heal from within, to learn from your mistakes and more importantly, loving your growth journey because it is *unique*. Vision is the ability to keep sowing, growing, learning, pruning and being present. It's being able to take those leaps of faith in the unexpected even when the current circumstances don't seem to be in alignment to your expectations. To add on this, it's crucial to make sure the expectations you have are suitable for your personal vision.

Abundant Progress

Don't run if you haven't learnt how to walk first. Life is in stages and will teach you how to start with humble beginnings.

The greater vision you have, the more disciplined and active you will be in feeding it with positivity, allowing the Lord to lead you to the right people and eventually start seeing opportunities of growth coming your way. Think about the time you had a vision to build something great; what steps did you initially take to keep it going? Was there any element of fear involved in the process, and if there was, how did you handle it? If the vision kept you on your feet, what did it teach you whilst seeing it grow and manifest? *#reflectivemoment.*

Your life won't always be what you expect it to be, but when you take the vision and leave it in the Maker's Hands, you will see how it germinates into abundance for His Glory. No matter what you build, remember that it can't be done alone. These are the uncomfortable moments where you need to keep pushing and the capacity of handling each season with balance. When building your vision, wisdom is involved – the ability to make decisions in a timely manner without looking back is a bonus and is how you are able to overcome clouded vision. There's nothing to go back to apart from embracing the past seasons for all it's put you through to be the person you are today.

A reminder for you: you are already doing well even when the results don't show. When you can't see your way clear, embrace the clouded visions for it is birthing greater faith and strength in you. You can still experience uncertainty and believe in what you desire to see happen!

THREE

THE COMPARISON TRAP

The world is full of 'what's next' moments. Rather than focusing on the present moment, our eager minds jump to the next season. No matter where you are right now, embrace every season that it's teaching you. I remember going to the British Library for an event in September 2021, and there were three panellists who spoke about their entrepreneurial journeys in their respective businesses. It was inspiring and they engaged very well with the audiences.

My key takeaway was the importance of focusing on what one of the entrepreneurs desired to achieve without the need to constantly look at what their competitors were doing. The entrepreneur believed in their vision and ran with it, yet inspired by the competition but not intimidated by it.

It's been said in the world of business that those who want to succeed should look at what their competitors are doing, including how to find the right marketing strategy, how to attract people with the right sales funnel on social media, how to increase market share, etc. Whilst all these components in business are important, I saw it as an opportunity to look within. How did I do this? By acknowledging that I must be accountable to my own journey of business, identifying opportunities of improvements and being open to collaborations that suit the vision and purpose of the business.

It is good when the community can celebrate your business' progress, but I want to remind you that when it's your time; it's your time, and no one can change that. In other words; what is for you, is for you. When you remember this, it will prevent you from being distracted and in turn, building your resilience and focus. It is a natural tendency to keep our eyes on what other people are doing as a sign to confirm whether we are in the right category. No one can

Abundant Progress

approve what you are doing apart from God and this comes through spending quality time with Him.

If you are anxious about tomorrow, it will rob you of today.

When it comes to abundant progress, it starts with your mind. Being easily swayed by pride can block opportunities of progress due to hiding mistakes and not wanting anyone to help you, and in turn, making it difficult to be genuinely happy for those that are doing well, not acknowledging the silent tears and moments they have gone through to achieve the next level. No matter what level you attain, there will always be a fight for it because nothing comes easy.

Do not be pressured in becoming successful without first understanding what your vision is and taking into account of your own progress. Vision may not always be clear at the early stages, however, with time, God reveals glimpses of what He requires of you. This takes constant work, effort and focus on your end to get to the stage where you finally say 'I surrender to Your Ways, Lord.'

There is no need to compare what God has not apportioned you to have with another individual. Why worry about what belongs to someone else? Your life and destiny aren't in the hands of anyone but God. Until you take the time to understand this, it will feel like a struggle. With patience and maturity, you will later realise that what you were looking for wasn't in God's Will for you in the first place. It was fear that caused you to act abruptly. There will come a stage in life where you will need to fight for what you desire and other moments where you need to be still.

Looking at life in the current season and comparing it with someone else is unwise because *comparing yourself with another person is idolising the individual.* You have to be confident to stay in your own lane and work on yourself. When it comes to life's opportunities and problems, particularly with what others are doing, you need to apply discernment and seek wisdom. Like King Solomon who didn't ask for wealth or the destruction of his enemies in 1 Kings 3:9, he acknowledged that all he desired was to have an understanding heart and would be able to discern good from evil.

Using discernment will change the course of your entire life.

Now it all makes sense when studying Genesis 1 about Adam and Eve in the Garden of Eden. Do you know the many problems faced in our world today is because of disobedience? Disobedience is what nearly separated us from the love of God, however, there was great grace and mercy given onto us. Jesus; the One who has no competitor is seated at the right-hand side of the Father, interceding for us and our mental health daily. You would be surprised at the protection God provides each day, yet we tend not to acknowledge it as much as we should.

No matter what your thoughts are, God wants them all. The life you live now reflects on how your future will look. How you operate today will correspond with your tomorrow. When it feels as if people are trying to rush you to 'get on with it' or 'you are moving too slow,' ask yourself **why**. Why do you need the pressure of listening to what others are saying about you? Yes, we have doubts and fears because we are human, but it doesn't mean we should stay the way we are.

When you try to fix things by yourself without the Holy Spirit guiding you, you will get hurt.

Surrender and work on yourself for you can't be your best self to others if you aren't your best self to you. When you are better to yourself, you control your moods, what you hear and what people say; being able to discern and listen before you speak. It is very important to know when to speak.

Don't let any unwholesome talk come out of your mouth, but only what is benefitting to the ears and valuable to your soul. Toxic

Abundant Progress

comparison can make you constantly vulnerable and eager to watch what other people are doing. When this becomes an occurrence, **pause**, and ask yourself if it's worth it because anything that steals your time and joy are liabilities.

No one is built to do life on their own, no matter who they are or how strong they look. Life becomes pleasurable when it is shared with others. We must learn how to listen to the stories that others have been through, understanding their journey and how we can contribute to it. It is so important to be intentional about the character you have and how you put yourself together even when plans aren't going the way you expected. Remember that your current situation isn't your permanent destination.

On the other hand, when you've been too strong for too long, it can make you withdraw from people and great opportunities. The more you do for others, the more you expect at some point to receive it back. Comparison doesn't start loudly. It is gentle in our thoughts and eventually starts running aimlessly. The power of having a positive mindset is through gratitude and genuinely celebrating people making you a trustworthy person. We shouldn't assume that our loved ones are changing because of decisions they decide to make in order to improve their mental well-being. Everyone you meet has a choice on who they want to be around. Take your time to pause and reflect. Think about the reasons why comparison happens according to the following points:

- **Family upbringing** – family lifestyle can be portrayed in so many ways, and this takes maturity to resolve it in a loving, yet firm manner. We didn't choose the families we are in presently. They were and still are gifts from above; gifts that we must cherish every second we have with them. It's not always easy understanding a parent's perspective unless you are willing and patient to understand their own upbringing in comparison to the 21st century millennial generation that has different viewpoints. We should be careful not to compare our family lifestyle to another family, for we are all uniquely

Abundant Progress

different. Not everyone may have the same privileges as another family, but it doesn't mean you are not valued.

- **Loss of identity** – when life takes you by surprise, it can cause you to question who you are, and ultimately make you operate in ways you shouldn't. Losing your identity causes dysfunction and makes you hungry for the world's approval. You don't need it because everything changes constantly. You want to place your identity in something that is stable, powerful and confident. When your identity is hidden in possessions, people-pleasing or pretending to be someone you are not, it eventually starts showing up in your character and mannerisms. Comparison should remind you of who you are; a fearfully and wonderfully made individual as Psalm 139:14 puts it. Your identity is in the One that made you.

- **Lack of encouragement** – when words are few, countless thoughts start to rise. The most important gifts that you will ever receive in your life isn't money or possessions, but the power of words. My love language is words of affirmation. When you are in a season of doubt, the greatest gift is when God provides someone to speak *into* your life, reminding you of the great future ahead. When you are tempted not to celebrate your loved ones when they receive good news, revert that back to yourself and ask if you would like to be treated that way. The words we speak to each other carry anointing and truth. Don't take the words spoken over your life lightly. Keep the good ones and disregard/reject the bad ones. Above all, don't wait for anyone to encourage you, but learn to encourage yourself in the Lord as David did in 1 Samuel 30:6.

- **Feeling socially isolated** – no matter who you are, there will be seasons in your life where you will feel alone from the crowd. It may be that nobody understands you which makes it difficult to open up. When that happens, practise controlling your emotions to avoid offence and anger in your heart, because it impacts on your health more than you know. Feeling socially isolated can be avoided when you communicate with the Father and tell Him everything that's on your heart; yes, He already knows what's happening in your life, but it is still good to open your mouth and speak. Whether through tears, journaling, or walking around your neighbourhood; they are all healthy for a balanced social lifestyle. Through your communication with God, He will start bringing the right people in your life to feed you with His wisdom and knowledge.

- **Not being understood** – this is difficult, especially when you are endeavouring to put your point across. Sometimes it may feel that people are taking you for granted causing questions to run through your mind. For example, you can give a gift to someone out of a good heart, but they seem ungrateful for the gift. It will cause you to question your good heart and wonder whether someone else would have appreciated it better. When you are misunderstood with a friend or family member, it takes strength, maturity and grace to handle the situation with respect. Knowing the right time to speak matters very much because we all handle circumstances differently. If you sense someone is not in the mood to speak, be patient, give them space, and when the time is ready, speak with ease and firmness as the other party may also need time to open up.

Our lives should elude love, unity, care and tenderness and we look at this from the Fruits of the Spirit in Galatians 5:22-23. It reads: "The fruit of the Spirit is love, joy, peace, patience, kindness, generosity, faithfulness, gentleness and self-control." Take a look at each component. Implementing these as part of your daily routine towards others is crucial and prevents the comparison trap from happening through discipline and application. These are all important fruits that must be shown through our character and the way we communicate.

It's not enough to stay the way you are and not take responsibility for nurturing the fruits in your life, for as a man thinks is his own heart, so is he in Proverbs 23:7. The way you think impacts you as an individual and causes others to treat you the way you treat yourself. There must a humble level of respect that you give yourself, especially when it comes to personal growth and the ability to remain stable despite what you see and how you feel. Your thoughts attract exactly what you say, which is why it's important to be patient when you are in seasons of testing.

Being confident regardless of what you are going through is not about bringing other people down, but being able to inspire and influence the minds of others in your environment that doesn't see anything good about themselves. I wrote a statement on my socials a few years back as a source of encouragement for those struggling with comparison. It reads:

"I love the fact that God did not create everyone to be the same, so you don't need to feel anxious about anything. It's such a heavy burden when it's easy for someone to look at another person assuming their life is better. This clouds your focus and puts you into secret battles within. Encourage yourself and don't wait for people to do it for you. Be true to who you are."

"Examine where you are right now. If you don't like it, change it. You are not alone in the battle. You don't want to be out of alignment but in the Will of God, knowing and hearing His voice on when to move. We don't live by how we feel. Emotions are temporal, so don't entertain them; instead, control them."

This statement has and will continue to help those that choose to apply what is written and make the relevant changes in their walk. You are confident in the One that's leading and guiding your steps each day despite what is happening around you. Your emotions are important, but don't give them any power to impact your faith; rather; use your faith to fuel your feelings into surrendering. No matter what season you are in, remember it is a *season* and life will change for the better if you allow the Author and Finisher of your faith to come in and dwell – Hebrews 12:2.

Abundant Progress

Be true to who you are, even when you don't feel like you're making progress. A life gradually led with God is better than a life based on short-cuts and having to start again. You don't want to entertain a quick-fix for temporal pleasure. You have to know the pace you can endure in order to achieve abundant progress. We must also be aware that progress isn't always measured by how much money we make at our workplaces or businesses, but being able to manage our mental and emotional health effectively, treating one another with respect and resonating with others in a healthy manner which are key factors.

When you are tempted to compare your season and it may not necessarily be with others; it could be a season you were in; for example, you preferred the year 2016 and constantly comparing it with 2019. There is a tendency that we have to ponder over what we liked about certain years and what didn't go well.

When we lack self-discipline, it becomes easier to focus on what hasn't yet happened because we dwell on 'the good days' and how we want them to come back, but it can be unhealthy if not analysed well. This is what Ecclesiastes 7:10 (NIV) emphasises which says: "Do not say 'why were the old days better than these?' for it is not wise to ask such questions." We must be mindful that each season teaches us great lessons that make us want to look forward, rather than dwell on past moments, making it difficult to see what is already ahead of you.

Being able to work on yourself by analysing your heart will contribute to the improvement stages. It's important to work on yourself first before trying to help others. The comparison trap can be avoided when you learn to thoroughly work on yourself, love who you are, including the season you are in, and maximising the gradual steps of the journey. Each day teaches you a lesson about who you are, and how to overcome certain struggles you may be facing, whether privately or publicly.

One of the greatest gifts you can give yourself and others is *the effectiveness of communication*. The majority of relationships that are successful and continues to grow strong is due to transparency

Abundant Progress

and openness. Asking the questions of; 'how are you doing?' or 'how has your mindset been lately?' makes the difference.

Waiting for the other person to respond when they are ready to speak is key as well. We have been through several moments of questioning whether we are doing enough – we have to be truthful and talk to ourselves about our character and discipline our emotions. There will be moments in life where you will have to leave certain situations and decide not to worry about the outcome. What you focus on magnifies. If you focus on someone else's progress without disciplining your emotions, it can cause you to second-guess yourself.

To add onto this, it's dangerous to be like someone else; no matter who you admire or want to aspire to become, don't make the mistake of wanting someone else's life because until you understand their pain, you don't want to set yourself up for disappointment. The experiences they've been through are there for us to learn from them. It is important to be inspired by what others in your environment are doing, but not to be solely fixated on every move they make, because what is working for them may not work for you. Comparison can expose vulnerabilities and flaws and this eventually starts from a place where you have to be intentionally honest with where you are and what isn't working in order to be free within.

Until we are real, we can't heal.

Most times, our greatest work isn't when we are always occupied with many tasks; it's when we truly realise that nothing can be done in our own strength and can't keep running to external sources for support or confirmation. It is through the leading of the Holy Spirit that we can operate successfully without the world convincing us otherwise. Whether you classify yourself as an influential individual, remember how much you had to go through to get the position of inspiring others authentically. Making it seem that it was

Abundant Progress

easy to get to the top paints a false perception of humility, and therefore, affects those around you.

Our society is constantly shouting 'validate me; support me' and at times, we can easily be influenced by what we see rather than what we know. Looking at other people won't take you to the place God longs for you to be in; the place of peace, solitude and contentment. He created desires for a reason, and those desires are not meant to take His place or cause us to compare ourselves so critically to others. Never make anyone an idol in your life, including your family or friends. We have all fallen and made plenty of mistakes. Instead, make an intentional decision to seek God and find out what He's called you to do and allow Him maximise the gradual steps of your own journey. This enables you to be yourself in the midst of coping with the changes that circumstances brings.

Your temporary season should teach you to invest in yourself and become better at making healthier decisions. Whether it's to stand out from the crowd and influence your community, that requires discipline and focus. When you appreciate who you are, you develop such a love that reflects from above. This shouldn't be taken lightly because the more you see yourself as God sees you, the opinions of others are nullified. Abundant progress can only start when you choose to accept who God has made you to be and work alongside Him. As He works on your heart, you are also improving in ways that you can't yet see. Changes happen in stages and when you hear testimonies of what other people had to overcome, it will ignite you to wait expectantly for your change to come.

The basic principles of a life filled with joy, gratitude and honour starts with appreciating where you are and not rushing to get to the next stage.

When you think of each day as it approaches, what comes to mind? Is it to start wandering on how the next two years will look, or are you allowing each day to flow organically? It's important for your mental well-being to control your thoughts that take away your

Abundant Progress

focus, time and attention from what is already in front of you. How many times have you focused on what you don't yet have, or felt complacent with where you are that you refuse to do anything else?

Decisions must be made and whether it is comfortable or not; it is still progress. Maximising the gradual steps requires a focused mind without the temptation to complain or procrastinate. The position you are in right now is what another person may desire without you realising. Remember what you desired has already come your way – don't forget all the good that's happened to you. You will never know how valuable your resources are until they are gone or replaced by someone else.

Still on the topic of comparison, what are you going to put in place to prevent your thoughts from thinking negatively:

_____

_____

_____

_____

_____

_____

Rather than competing, we grow better when complements of strength are given and the desire to see change in the other person. Question: 'What does competing achieve in my life?' A bold individual is able to work on themselves without the opinions of what others say. They are able to take what works for them and refuse to accept what isn't for them. Not everything that is spoken of needs a reaction.

Abundant Progress

Observation is a powerful component when getting to know new people in different environments; gradually, you will be able to identify who you need. Attending an event of 20 guests or more may end up with two organic connections out of the rest, and that is totally fine. On the other hand, you may have attended the event and wasn't able to connect with anyone. Remember, nothing in life should be forced, and those who enjoy who you are will connect with you organically. This is not the time to fit in and want everyone to work with you. You are called for a specific audience.

Consider complementing one another rather than competing with one another.

We should be mindful that we don't end up having ulterior motives for what we do. No one knows what tomorrow will hold and doing good opens up great opportunities that wouldn't have been possible if done in isolation. No matter who you are, you need the right people and this starts with how you see yourself and how relatable you are around others. Can people trust you? Can people see your genuineness?

These attributes matter to all of us regardless of how much one has achieved. It is not an excuse to use your accolades as an opportunity to treat others unfairly. It takes grace to be focused on your own journey and inspire others, rather than being put off by another person's achievements. One of the key lessons about perception will always be in how God reminds you to see yourself in Him because you are a reflection of His character. He shapes you through discipline. You may fail the test and start again, but that is His love for you. He wants you to get it right, no matter how many times you fall. His best for you is greater than anyone else and you know it.

When you stop believing in your vision, you will distract yourself by watching others and end up starting again. Appreciating the skills, talents and gifts you have is a responsibility that must be handled with care. Do not take your life or anything given for granted – you'll never know how effective you will be until you

Abundant Progress

work it to the best of your ability. Have you put all the effort into the task or are you taking it slow and steady?

A life of abundance isn't for the swift so take your time and focus on the areas in your life that you are intentional on seeing change. The changes that you don't see straight away are pruning your character. Before abundance comes, the way you handle people, money, wealth, relationships and your health will indicate how far you will go. In addition to this, the way you treat people is a reflection of how you treat yourself; don't take this lightly, especially as opportunities will start finding you, because they will. Understand that we are all in different seasons and maturity stages. What you learn from another person could be helping you become better.

No matter what other people are doing at this time, let that be an inspiration for you to build on an abundant mindset and keep soaring. When you walk with God, He will guide and lead you on what to say, where to go and what to do with your season. When you trust and follow His leading, it will start becoming more easier when identifying with opportunities that are and aren't for you.

If you have experienced unhealthy comparison, how did you identify it and what solutions did you put in place to prevent it from affecting others?

_____

_____

_____

_____

_____

_____

Abundant Progress

We all have secret battles; some more painful than others, and for this reason, being sensitive to the Holy Spirit will help to calm the situation. Your words are vital and what you say is what you'll have. The power of what you say can either make or break a situation, so it is important to be very mindful of the thoughts you think about. Matthew 15:11 helps us to understand that what goes into someone's mouth doesn't defile them, but what comes out of their mouth is what defiles them.

The more abundant you become, the more limited your speech must be.

Don't talk anyhow because you want to. Speak in wisdom and at the right time. The words that are to be spoken aren't meant to be for pulling yourself or others down, but making an intentional decision to overcome your fears one step at a time. When you encounter a dream or vision about abundance, what comes to mind? Do you accept it or reject it? The first step is to write the dream down in your journal or diary so that you remember it when moments of uncertainty come. We can use uncertainty to make us focus on what matters which is how we are treating our minds.

Having a positive mindset is a gift that once nurtured well, it becomes easier for people to gravitate towards you. Living in an imperfect world causes us to remember this and cautions us carefully about our words, our deeds, our works and our commitment to what we do and what we believe in. I refuse to allow my thoughts to be controlled by what I see, rather; I discipline the mind to ensure that it's in alignment to the Will of God and continue walking boldly to where He has entrusted me.

Don't let comparison be bigger than your prayer life. Being honest and open in wisdom about your struggles will eventually become a source of strength. Those moments are what propels you to keep on moving forwards. You always want to look back and thank the past for the lessons it taught you, because what you learn in the hard

Abundant Progress

times propels you to keep going. The late Maya Angelou said **'And still I RISE!'** which came from her poem 'Still I Rise' sharing her experiences about survival and hope in 1978. *Source: <https://www.biography.com/news/maya-angelou-still-i-rise>.*

It becomes more powerful when stories are shared during moments where it became difficult to move on. Your story will always be an inspiration to the person that listens to your podcast or reads your book. Don't underestimate the power of your life and the experiences encountered because it is strengthening people more than you'll ever know. We may feel tempted to pretend that our lives are perfect and nothing is troubling us, however, keeping it in and not sharing it is what makes it difficult to resonate with others. You don't have to go through any situation alone; it will take strength, time, grace and patience to eventually let it all out, but it will help to work on your journey with gradual ease.

Looking at what others are doing and comparing it to your life will deter you from focusing on what's already in front of you. The right people will find you when you change the way you think about yourself. Work on your heart and let each day teach you a lesson of greatness, despite what you haven't yet been able to achieve. There's a reason why life is called the journey, and **not** the final destination.

A reminder for you: Your life is unique. You are not like anyone else. Let your choices complement your surroundings and uplift others. Life is not a race; it is a journey, so enjoy it whilst you have the time. The only competition you have is to keep on becoming stronger and better at making wise choices than you did yesterday. As Psalm 31:19 puts it; *how abundant are the good things that God has stored up for those who fear Him!* Let your focus be on the One that has access to the abundant life you desire, therefore, eliminating all forms of unhealthy comparison.

FOUR

UNEXPECTED BREAKTHROUGH

It's when you least expect it that God comes through and surprises you! God is and always will be faithful. I want to bring you to a place of meditation. When was the last time you cried? As in, deeply cried where you felt breathless? Those tears that've been waiting to be released from your eyes – it is a part of life, and no matter who you are, we will all get to the stage where we are burned out, however, this is where the reflective pause comes in and ultimately, taking healthy rest and renewal.

Unexpected breakthroughs are for those who are positioned, ready and expectant to receive, no matter what they see or don't see. It's about shifting your mindset to believe in better, but the key is always applying what you know through the Word of God in order for the door to be opened. No matter what season you are in, life can be uncomfortable, and although some are gifted at handling their moments with grace, you still have every right to make it through and with patience, you will overcome.

Being joyful is a strong sign of expectation for a breakthrough, and we should know by now that joy is contagious. Even when life doesn't always work out the way you expected, you know that your identity is not in your circumstances but in who God called you to be. This is the joy that we get when we know that all things are working together for our good – Romans 8:28.

There is a season and a time for unexpected breakthroughs to occur and this includes opportunities that you didn't look for. It will take patience, grace and the ability to work on your pace to understand that owning your season brings gradual progress, allowing you to not only learn from your mistakes, but receive the best that God has for you.

Abundant Progress

Within the month of February 2022, I felt in my spirit such peace that when everything is submitted to God without worry or fear, it will bring the multiplication. God doesn't want any of His children to have a weak mindset, but to believe that when they put their desires in His Hands, He will turn it around and make it exceedingly and abundantly beautiful. It really made me smile that evening and I knew that God was constantly speaking about the beauty of seasons and how He is involved in all of them, not missing any out.

When your spirit matches up with your faith, it brings greater blessings and testimonies.

To be spiritually mature takes heart work as it requires eradicating every distraction that weighs you down and instead, building strength from every opposition. How you cope with delays whilst maintaining a positive attitude will prepare you for the unexpected breakthrough. In Exodus 3:8, the emphasis is on the **milk** and **honey**. What draws me to this scripture is where it says: "So, I have come down to deliver them from the power of the Egyptians, and to bring them up from that land to a good and spacious land, to a land flowing with milk and honey." The following providential blessings can be applied in every area of your life, from personal achievements, to character-building, business & financial stability, and healthy relationships & friendships within the community:

- **Abundance**
- **Increase**
- **Provision**
- **Acceleration**
- **Growth**

We must understand that the spirit of prosperity comes from the One who knows where you are at this time and what you can handle. Rushing your way through to obtain the prize will cause you to start

Abundant Progress

again. **Reminder**: Do not underestimate or question why life isn't working the way you expected it to. There are delays for your own good to protect and make you humble.

A blessing that is given too soon isn't a blessing at all and can cause one to misuse it without applying wisdom. There is pressure to perform in our millennial generation and not enough time to meditate and reflect. Our focus is constantly on how we can attain the levels we desire to be in without first realising that it takes time to build.

Having abundance requires consistency and relentlessness in order to increase the capacity on how your mindset works, so that you are able to multiply and accelerate which ultimately leads to growth. Doing what naturally comes best to you is attractive rather than trying to do more than expected. If it is not your gifting, don't tamper with it. Let your gifts naturally unfold.

There are moments in our lives where we may be eager to do what society deems as successful, but when you try it, it doesn't seem to work. Being hard on yourself is not your portion and doesn't contribute to the beauty God created you to be. I am aware that nothing successful can be done alone, however, being in a season of stillness prepares you for the breakthrough. Trying to fix or build your way to the top without understanding the purpose behind your acceleration will cause confusion.

In as much as we shout about receiving unexpected breakthroughs, we must learn to discern what is coming our way and whether it is coming from God or our desires. For example, an opportunity to become a writing contributor for a creative individual can seem like the perfect fit, but just because it looks like a great opportunity doesn't mean it is for you. Having received an email invitation from a company that wanted me to be part of their team, I decided to do further research on the company, their values, what they stand for and how active they were on their socials.

I wasn't convinced enough and decided to ask the individual that emailed me to have a Zoom meeting so as to discuss further what

Abundant Progress

the opportunity consisted of. The response I received back was the same format as the first email and a link to fill out my details to get a response within 24 hours.

I prayed over it and replied to the company to suggest a Zoom meeting and didn't hear from them again. This was when I knew it wasn't genuine. When opportunities come your way, it is **your responsibility** to take time and find out why they want you to work for them, rather than agreeing with anything that is given to you.

Be specific and know what you want, or other people will make you into who they want you to be. This unexpected breakthrough was a real wake-up call to understand that not everything that looks good is for you, and the reputation you have is dependent on who you are surrounded with and who you work alongside.

Don't allow excitement to make you rush into decisions you aren't ready to take responsibility of.

Our unexpected breakthroughs can either teach us lessons, confirm to us what we've been waiting years for, or develop a stronger prayer life. Be what God has called you to be, and remain firm in that decision. Make peace with where you are rather than wanting to know what is next in your life and leaving the outcome to God. You won't enjoy life if you were to know every detail; this is why our faith is highly vital to have in every season. There are reasons why certain projects, careers, relationships, friendships and opportunities didn't work out when you wanted them to. Instead, discipline your mind to learn from your current situation and let it naturally unfold.

One of the joys I've realised whilst writing and taking each day as it comes is that:

- You won't always realise that you are in a new season completely.
- It takes time to make peace with where you are and accept your season.

Abundant Progress

- Just like we have winter, spring, summer and autumn, each quarter of the year changes; sometimes for the better; other times, to challenge our thoughts to overcome certain barriers.

Unexpected breakthroughs can work in both ways in the good times and challenging moments. Society has played a major role on being vaguely **transparent** with a touch of **authenticity**. In uncertainty, it's crucial that honesty and integrity play a vital role to what you portray in public because you'll never know who is watching. Don't underestimate where you are because it doesn't seem like anything is working. You can build in silence and wait in patient expectation that your seed will grow and produce good fruit.

In as much as unexpected breakthroughs can occur at any time, it also requires you to understand the different seasons you are in. There are some breakthroughs that can't happen in certain environments that aren't pleasant. Spiritually, we have to be wise, discerning and extremely prayerful wherever we go, who we surround ourselves with and the churches, networking events, and the opportunities we are invited to.

Not every opportunity that is revealed is for you, and you have the right to decline. If you have been in the same season for a while, take quality time out and ask yourself what is going on. Speak to God and ask Him to reveal the delays and what is blocking you from moving forwards.

There are moments where you also need to enjoy your own company. Resist the urge to please people on social media and spend quality time offline. When you least expect it, the breakthroughs will gradually start to show in your conversations, those who you choose to connect with and being able to make bold decisions unapologetically. We all at some stage require to see REAL CHANGE in our lives.

Staying on the same level is not healthy and choosing to accept life the way it is becomes a challenge, not just for yourself, but the future

Abundant Progress

generation. Abundance starts in the mind, but it can also be taken away when the environment does not match up with your faith. Specific desires are blessings or opportunities that we are intentional about seeing come to fruition, but this kind can only come with prayer and fasting in reference to Matthew 17:21. When you are desperate to see a transformation, there are decisions that must be made without the approval of others. Whether they like it or not, they are not going where God is taking you, so **don't be distracted**.

Let me take you on a journey to the experience of *fasting to breakthrough*. 2021 was a great year in terms of spiritual development, growth and insight. With many revelations of seeking God, resisting snacks, partaking in the Daniel Fast for the first time, and having a rich encounter with God put many things into perspective.

Fasting deepened my relationship and showed me what God wanted me to see, from my personal prayers that were met, to chains of bondage being broken over my life. Through tears, time off social media, and soaking myself in the Word of God as well as listening to sermons, I was enlightened, encouraged and disciplined to see the changes that took place all the while.

I did not know what to expect, but I knew that something had to break! There were days where it became heavy and various enemies thought they succeeded in weighing my spirit down, however, through the fast, I was sharply focused on my purpose, the goals that God set out for me to fulfil and the ability to discern wisely.

God gives visions to inform His children of the blessings that are yet to come.

We should be aware that fasting is spiritually nourishing and being able to bask in His Presence and taking our relationship with the Lord seriously, is what enables Him to move on our behalf. However, be mindful that a transactional relationship is not what God wants; we want to seek His Face and not only His Hands or what He can offer us. The power of prayer and fasting always has

Abundant Progress

great influence. I started seeing changes and leaps of faith, from doubt to believing for the impossible! I would hear testimonies of individuals buying cars without a secured job, and a few weeks later, God providing stable job positions, from other individuals that read newspapers and viewed houses they were keen to enquire of, to visiting and declaring it was their own! It seemed crazy, but when you put your faith to the test with fasting the right way (further study on true fasting is based in Isaiah 58:3-10), it will produce double the results of what you couldn't do on your own. This is why we can't work in our own strength; we need the supernatural power of God to intervene for us when we are weak.

You have to get to the stage where you say 'enough is enough!'

Being a cheerful giver also contributes to gradual success because God encourages us to give generously. Your contributions towards others can be in many ways from finances, being a source of encouragement, speaking words of life over someone's situation, visiting a loved one who is unwell, cooking food for your family, cleaning around the house, and interceding for others when they are in need. As you continue to help other people, God is preparing something that's bigger than you. He is able to trust you because you put His needs first.

You may be in a season of constant sowing, giving, or encouraging others, but don't yet see the harvest. Hebrews 6:10 and Galatians 6:9 are similar scriptures reminding us that God is not unjust and will not forget your work of love you have shown Him as you help His people and not becoming tired of doing good.

You may feel underestimated when you are constantly giving out your time, support and contributions, but a season is coming where you will reap all that you've invested. I refused to hold back and supported freely wherever I could at the appropriate time, with the leading of the Holy Spirit. Through this, opportunities that were

Abundant Progress

birthed enabled me to gain strength and build more confidence in Him making me fully dependent on His Word.

It's the gradual steps that's made the journey worthwhile and learning how to enjoy the beauty of the process. Unexpected breakthroughs aren't always about what you can get from the other person; it is about God showing you His Will and being obedient to it. To add on, The Parable of the Sower also correlates with chapter 7 that deals with *faith* which we shall go into very soon. However, unexpected breakthroughs are shown in many ways, not only through faith, but in sowing, reaping and harvesting. Let's take a look at Matthew 13:18-23 (NIV) in further depth:

"Listen then to what the parable of the sower means:

[19] When anyone hears the message about the Kingdom and does not understand it, the evil one comes and snatches away what was sown in their heart. This is the seed sown along the path:

[20] The seed falling on rocky ground refers to someone who hears the word and at once, receives it with joy.

[21] But since they have no root, they last only a short time. When trouble or persecution comes because of the word, they quickly fall away.

[22] The seed falling among the thorns refers to someone who hears the word, but the worries of this life and the deceitfulness of wealth choke the word, making it unfruitful.

[23] But the seed falling on good soil refers to someone who hears the word and understands it. This is the one who produces a crop, yielding a hundred, sixty or thirty times what was sown." When given an instruction to obey and believe, it starts with an unshakable mindset before it becomes a reality. There will be moments where unexpected breakthroughs will occur, however, being positioned accordingly will enable you to be in alignment to God's Will and

Abundant Progress

not miss out. In the table below, read the three options and tick the relevant box that represents you at this time:

1. You've been given a word of encouragement to remind you to keep going. You strive to believe and, on several occasions, you are excited, however, when external pressure and countless fears start going through your mind, the encouragement loses its grip due to your foundation being shaky.	
2. When a word of encouragement is given, it becomes difficult to accept it because of the way you see life which has a negative impact on your relationship with faith to believe for change. You are still holding onto Plan B in case Plan A doesn't work.	
3. Despite what is currently happening in your life, you are intentional about building faith through the Word of God and is confident that the harvest is already here. You have been faithful with what's in your hands and learning the importance of multiplication. You constantly seek God first and gain strength to keep going. Through this, you see the fruits from your initial investment.	

*No matter which option you chose, it's the honesty that brings freedom**

Having an abundant life starts with your mind and the intentional decision to say 'I am ready for change' – not only speaking it, but becoming the individual who remains faithful to the call and understands the power that the Word has over their lives which therefore enables them to produce multiple harvests. What you put in is what you get out, and this includes the time we spend with God. Having a lifetime of abundance starts with God and not what is seen externally, neither does it involve the opinions of others, but being in God's Presence and allowing Him to will show you where your life is heading to.

Abundant Progress

The unforeseen breakthrough moments were when I least expected it.

Breakthrough moments are silent and unannounced which starts in your spirit. You have to believe even when you are praying and nothing seems to be changing. All you can do is encourage yourself in the Lord as David did in 1 Samuel 30:6 and laugh hilariously like Sarah did when God promised her a child at an old age in Genesis 18:12. These are both unforeseen blessings and when you study these two key scriptures, you will see how God moved mightily in their lives to bring forth multiple and generational breakthroughs that were so vast.

The power of tears releases tension that needs a place to let the emotions out and anything that's causing you to become dysfunctional must be dealt with wisely. When there are constant breakdowns, know that a time will come where you will look back and laugh at all the problems that once caused disappointment. As mentioned previously, laughter is a very great sentiment that is used to exude joy.

Laughter is one of my greatest medicines! Being able to control the way I respond to situations has enabled me to keep a joyful heart, even when it would have been easier to complain and become bitter about life. Choosing to see the best in every situation is a mindset skill that must be implemented each day.

As mentioned in chapter 3 about the comparison trap, the importance of words are vital for abundance and progress put together. When you think about words, envision them as seeds. You plant them in the soil and eventually end up being responsible for nurturing them.

As you are speaking, remember that words follow and will impact your environment. When you think small, you get small and when

Abundant Progress

you think big, you get big. It is important, however, to think gradually and not force anything to happen when it's not yet time.

The multiplication is in the worship – Being able to lay aside every weight and focus on the One that knows how to lift those heavy burdens from your life. The power of worship brings the breakthrough and I remember a time where all I could was to constantly seek God in my prayer room. With hands stretched upwards and kneeling, all I could do was allow the tears to roll down my face and exclaim how worthy He is. This wasn't the time to send a long list of what I wanted, but to take time out of the day to appreciate the greatness of God in my life.

The times where it seemed that God wasn't acknowledged enough in my life, caused me to serve Him more; the time will come where nothing you have or are yet desiring will ever compare to the Presence of God. No wonder why Psalmist David exclaimed in Proverbs 16:11 that in His presence, there is fullness of joy and at His Right Hand, there are pleasures forevermore. This shows that all David wanted was to please the Father and seek His strength for the times He'd faced intense battles.

When your focus is not on your wants and needs, but on how to please God and become acquainted with Him, that is where unexpected breakthrough will occur, particularly opportunities you didn't ask for. We ought to learn key lessons from our ancestors and understand how they dealt with life, and how we too, can deal with our own wisely.

Even when it seemed that my plans didn't go the way I expected, there was still hope that I held onto. When it became difficult to see my way clear, praise and thanksgiving started to rise up within, even when it felt lonely at times and more comfortable to stay silent, I chose to overcome by reminding myself and others why it is important to believe that their breakthrough is on the way.

Psalm 72:16 reminds us that our blessings shall surely abound throughout the land and on top of the hills, that our crops will

Abundant Progress

flourish like Lebanon and therefore, thrive like the grass of the field. This is what we must continue to hold onto even when it seems that nothing is changing.

It is our patience that attracts the unexpected breakthroughs, and what you don't put pressure on will eventually birth beautiful blessings that will ripen in due season. No matter how it looks right now, I have been there. The times where you wonder whether God will come through; the moments where you spent time constantly worrying and not giving yourself the time to rest.

No matter who you are, I want to encourage you that when the doubts come in like a flood, respond with joy and believe in the promises. Don't wait until your life starts to blossom before you step into your blessings. Life won't be perfect, but you can expect every imperfect season to work for your utmost good.

A reminder for you: When you don't focus on what you desire and keep active on the task in front of you, that is where abundance will come looking for you. There is a time and season for everything; to seek, to search, but also to rest, to trust and to be expectant. Unexpected breakthrough is coming for you – be prepared; be ready!

FIVE

THE ART OF GRATITUDE

Sometimes, we forget that the most powerful attribute to having a great life of abundance is **gratitude!** The art of gratitude is a heart posture, especially when we hear testimonies and stories of how people overcame certain obstacles. You wouldn't understand the depth of someone's journey until you relate to their pain, because it's easy to celebrate others when they are excelling. There is a natural connection to associate ourselves with those that are doing well, and although this is good, it doesn't mean that you should doubt your growth and neglect your season. There still needs to be gratitude in every situation.

The progress you have on earth is shown through consistency, patience and hard work; all internal blessings that are important for others to see the fruit that God has placed in you to blossom. Of course, not everything we want to have will come at once, but if you don't know how to appreciate the season you are in, life will teach you about it. I've learnt in every situation, to thank God, especially for the gift of life.

When you wake up in the morning without no pain and can function effectively, it makes you appreciate everything around you, including nature. When you hear the birds chirping early in the morning or embracing those long walks at night in the cool breeze; how beautiful is that! We must learn how to be still and enjoy nature.

During seasons of waiting and being expectant for change to come, I decided to be grateful for all the blessings around me, because an ungrateful heart leads to heartache. I couldn't stand being a complainer and wanted to create positivity within my environment. I was intentional to make sure that when people were around me, they would feel a sense of thankfulness, peace and openness.

Abundant Progress

There will be moments where you will have to appreciate everything in your reach, and this is what I participated in during the lockdown season. It didn't matter what wasn't available to me at the time; what mattered to me was how much God's love constantly takes care of His own. The blessings that we don't deserve is granted to us because of God's nature which is *love*. He saw you in your broken state and chose you to be His own, enabling you to achieve more than you could even think of.

The purpose of gratitude is to appreciate everything God's given you.

If you are in the season of complaining, there is a healthy way to express it. When I think about David and his eloquence in writing the Psalms, I was intrigued by his triumphs, successes, honesty and vulnerability about being real with God in his high and low moments. It is healthy to honour how we feel and yet, have a thankful heart for how far God has brought us. The journey of life won't always be easy, but when you have a heart of thanksgiving, it makes all the difference.

I took some time out of the day to tune into the Desiring God's podcast. The speaker was Greg Morse and he shared these profound words:

"Want what you already have. Don't slave to make your bank account rise to match your desires, but bring your desires down to match what God has put in your bank account. He reminds us that the answer to happiness is not bigger and better, but simpler and more grateful. Keep your life free from love of money and be content with what you have."

No matter how much you have, life will never satisfy you, so learn to be joyful with your portion. You must learn to discipline yourself to not only work with what you have, but avoid looking at what other people are doing and complaining about it. Your work ethic won't

Abundant Progress

be the same as another person, and the joy of this is knowing that you are unique.

That's why there are some people who have less but are able to utilise what they have well because they've positioned themselves to be thankful and have made it work well to their advantage. In all things, no matter what you do or don't have, be grateful. Don't allow the void in your heart to cause you to become selective on what you appreciate and what you won't appreciate.

In all seasons, we are encouraged to be thankful as 1 Thessalonians 5:18 says. Apostle Paul encouraged the Thessalonian church to remain thankful despite what they were going through. Some seasons prepare you for what is ahead, and other seasons make you slow down and focus on one task at a time. More importantly, every season reminds you not to rush the preciousness of life, and to love every moment where you are learning and evolving. Where you are now isn't your final destination, so don't remain complacent. When you need to move, do so.

Before you see change in the working environment, you must appreciate the management team for seeing value in you and accepting you for the job role. In order to see business growth, you must learn to cherish and value your customers and clients who choose to work with you. Everyone in life has a decision to make, and it's up to you to make it work for your good. How this works is by being thankful for those around you. There should never be a time where you don't need anyone. No matter who you are, life can't be done alone. We must learn to enjoy the steps of life and make the most of it with gratitude.

Take time to do something completely different. If you haven't visited your neighbour before, why not take the time out to cook a meal and offer it to them? See how their reaction would be. It's the small gestures that makes the greatest impact. If you are constantly on the receiving end and aren't used to giving out to others, givers will eventually burn out and stop. You must understand that having an abundant and progressive life is about reciprocation. Remember

Abundant Progress

that Galatians 6:9 encourages us to never stop doing good because it will come back at the appointed time.

We may not always be exposed to everything that happens around the world, but there is beauty in being able to appreciate where you are and focus on your own season; the opportunity to live in a warm home; yes, it may not be as fancy as you'd want it to be, but it's still a home which in the near future, you can renovate. There is nothing impossible that can't be achieved; it's about maintaining a positive attitude and being in the present moment.

The joys of being positive adds to your beauty and character. Being able to understand the ways in which you are around people is another contributing factor of expressing great gratitude. Examine and thank God for the amazing people He's placed in your life that's contributed to your growth and development.

On the other hand, before anyone can make you joyful, you must learn how to be joyful within. When someone is constantly complaining about their life and not doing anything about it, there will come a time where letting the person go in love will relieve you, especially when you have done all you can to support the individual. Do not take the responsibility of another person if they aren't willing to support themselves.

Being positive is not a temporal feeling; it is an intentional mindset shift!

Your mindset is powerful and how you think is determined by the words that are spoken. You must understand that everyone is going through changes. It's the art of gratitude that develops character and lifestyle because anyone can be thankful in good seasons, but when you don't see results the way you expected, how you respond determines your attitude.

Snapping back or becoming resentful when plans don't go your way will delay your progress. It's important to have moments where you

Abundant Progress

look back over your life and be thankful for the key lessons learnt throughout the process. This enables you to see your way clear to avoid procrastination.

When it comes to being still, it refers to self-control – ensuring that your mind isn't going any further than today. Today is today. Tomorrow is tomorrow. Focus on one day at a time and work with what you have. This enables you to be still in the present moment and is therapeutic, attractive and contributes to your well-being. It is wise to make decisions that don't always involve others; rather, applying Matthew 6:33 in every situation and inviting the Holy Spirit to dwell in you.

Your thoughts, actions, and habits are in alignment, and being able to honour the One that knows you is a powerful attribute to unexpected breakthroughs, because you know that all along, if it wasn't for God that was on your side, you would have been destroyed in reference to Psalm 124:2. When was the last time you complained? Be free to express yourself below:

I complained about...

_____

_____

_____

_____

_____

_____

_____

Abundant Progress

What did you *do* about your complaint?

_____
_____
_____
_____
_____

What practical steps will you put in place to stop complaining going forwards?

_____
_____
_____
_____
_____

Don't hold back when it comes to how you are feeling at a set moment in time; letting it out eventually leads to a refreshing

Abundant Progress

moment of thanksgiving and the beauty of gratitude will start becoming more obvious in your life. Through the difficult times and rejected moments, choose to pick yourself up and keep your heart at rest by not allowing it to wander on many thoughts at once.

The more thankful you are, the greater peace you will have with those around you and they will start to see gradual changes in you that will inspire them to live a life of gratitude. We are not to be those who are only thankful when life becomes easier, but we can be thankful in the difficult moments as well.

You are able to stand the fire when you've been through a lot and is able to say 'though I am slayed, I will still trust in the Lord' as Job stated in Job 13:15. Can you be thankful when everything is lost? Can you be thankful when it seems like everything you are trying to build just doesn't seem to work?

Remember that your thankfulness will extend to those around you, whether you realise it or not. You are meant to live a life of influence and be the light into a dark world so that people will see the Glory of God in you. Every step we make and move we take is for the benefit of the Kingdom and the lives of those who are yet to discover you.

The way you apply body lotion, apply gratitude to every area of your life.

If everything was given to you without toil or you didn't struggle or contribute anything to it, you are more likely to end up taking it for granted. Thankfulness and gratitude are powerful heart and mind postures. I strongly believe that the sufferings we encounter strengthen and enable us to be thankful for the good times that are ahead. Each day reminds us that no matter who we are; the status, occupation, influence or position one is in, doesn't exclude them from life's challenges. The more thankful I became, the more opportunities came my way to reaffirm that a grateful heart is essentially important to your physical, emotional and mental health.

Abundant Progress

To add onto this, being awarded at the Wise Women Awards Ceremony in March 2022 for Christian Book of the Year was a humbling opportunity, and all I could do was thank God for allowing me to come this far with the writing journey. Moments like this deserve so much thanksgiving because of God's favour, and I encourage you today, to keep being thankful because what you do now will eventually produce an abundant harvest.

A word of encouragement: May your life be a reflection of how important it is to trust God, and may He lift you higher to bring more people to Him, causing them to trust in His unfailing works and love. He is very worth depending on and will do more than you expect in your life too.

When we forget the great lessons and blessings that we've been given, it eventually starts to have an impact on the way life is heading. No matter what you are going through, remember that a lifestyle of gratitude shows in your speech and conduct. You may not have what you need right now, but it shouldn't stop you from reaching out in thanksgiving and be grateful for your lot.

It's even the smallest lessons you learn in private that help you to be more thankful than being celebrated for a good work ethic. I've learnt in the silent seasons that my gratitude speaks for me, especially when God places people in my life that I wouldn't have expected to receive.

Living an abundant life requires greater intimacy and time well-spent with the Father, so that He can tell you what to do and where to go on how to secure opportunities. The lessons that are learnt can take a lifetime to master, making it effective to continually seek God for guidance and direction. No matter what you have achieved, you still need the right mindset and attitude of thankfulness.

God could have chosen anyone else to build an empire, but He chose you. He sees the heart you have to give, and therefore, is able to trust that what you do with the gifts will expand and multiply the

Abundant Progress

Kingdom. Be intentional about the consistency of gratitude because it can take you further than working in your own strength.

It may take time to be thankful due to past pain and unhealed wounds, but it is still an attitude that must be carried out each day to have peace of mind and stillness. Through the calmness of life, that is where you are able to reflect on the goodness of God, and despite how imperfect life is, there is an opportunity to keep moving on gracefully in gratitude. Although there are times in life where venting seems easy to come by, maximising the steps of the journey starts with what you've learnt in the process and how you can utilise it to be better.

Our obstacles can be magnified when we give it too much attention.

You may be in a season where nothing is happening and everything looks the same, but through your gratitude, it will open up opportunities that rejection letters eventually become redirection letters of acceptance. Do not underestimate the power of a 'thank you.' Have integrity in your heart to serve others and help them where you can. When God starts bringing abundant opportunities your way, are you quick to announce it on social media or do you first of all, thank Him for the pathway He made?

Announcing God's goodness is an opportunity to keep going and allow others around you to be inspired to increase their faith. When you are inspired by the journey of your friends, that should position you to be more expectant and cause you to celebrate what God is doing in their lives. This is why life will always be in stages because what you learn in one season can be developed in another. It is important not to forfeit what the current season is teaching you because of what you are desiring.

If what you desire isn't going to benefit the Kingdom or help the community, it will most likely end up being in vain, and anything done to bring praise onto thyself is pride in the eyes of the Lord.

Abundant Progress

Don't let this be you. When what you desire is more than the God who gave it to you, it will eventually become an idol and distraction, and if you can't be content with what you have, how will you be able to handle more?

Don't underestimate the importance of small steps because they end up birthing great results when you learn to apply patience. You never want to have a blessing that is difficult to manage, so be humble and remain consistently thankful. The more gratitude you have, the better equipped you will be for the next stage of life. Think about it this way; when you look at the different shades of colour for art, what does it remind you of?

In secondary school, art was one of my favourite subjects. Each day, I see art as not only a blessing but freedom of gratitude; the bold and natural colours that work well together, and the beauty it brings to pictures and videos are outstanding, especially in museums and exhibitions.

What makes you smile has a lot to do with your perceptions about life. What creates gratitude has to do with how far God has brought you. Life is not a race; it is a journey, and you are always evolving, whether you see it or not. Life does not end when your needs have been met, because no matter what you have now, there's an eagerness to want more.

Having more abundance requires self-discipline, a consistent work ethic and the ability to work well under pressure. When you are able to utilise these key tools, alongside being grateful for where you are, you will understand why certain moments in your life took a while to manifest. Decisions will have to be made where looking after your own internal needs becomes more of a priority than possessions.

Abundant wealth is peace, joy, calmness and loving the season you are in.

Abundant Progress

Even when small blessings appear, you still need to be grateful because how you handle small blessings will indicate how you'll manage bigger expectations. Abundant progress is preparing you for greatness, but in order to confidently receive what God has for you, it is important to prepare privately in prayer. For opportunities to speak with a number of people, it will require going through notes and practising, speaking with your mentors, family members or loved ones, setting yourself free from disappointments and ultimately, forgiving others as well as yourself.

There is power in connections and smart networking. When someone comes into your life and they are happy you are in theirs, that is an opportunity to show them gratitude. As the saying goes – 'your network is your net-worth' and I stand on this greatly. Look around and see the people who are in your life that cause you to grow wisely and make the right choices.

We are required to work effectively with others and sharpen their skills to create greater opportunities. Although not everyone will be in your life forever, there are still key lessons that can be learnt from having their presence around. You can look back over your life and be thankful that someone took their time to invest in your well-being to be where you are today.

There are greater opportunities to be thankful for especially the moments where certain needs weren't answered. At that moment in time, it felt painful trusting in the person you thought would help along your journey, or the 20-page application form to get the promotion at work, but you learnt more from the rejection; your tenacity increased and you didn't lose hope in God or yourself.

Instead, you made it by walking above and beyond and continuing on your journey of gratitude. God had to close that chapter in your life because He knew you weren't going to be happy in the years to come. When the hard times come, remember that rejection is what makes you stronger and dependent on the One that knows your life.

We will have to get to a stage where reflection becomes a consistent habit to understand why the beauty in certain situations occur.

Abundant Progress

Through it all, we are taught how to give God thanks. This is why the story about The Prodigal Son in Luke 15:11-32 is a rich reminder of what it is to be thankful whilst reflecting on the unconditional love of a Father.

Each time I study the story about The Prodigal Son and his disobedience towards his father, it makes me realise how impatient we can be. With impatience comes ingratitude where we only want to be thankful when we have our own way met.

Discontentment leads to a complacent spirit and divided focus. For this reason, when we are eager to gain a certain status, whether it's wanting to prove to others that put you down that you are more successful than them, it eventually leads to pride which starts off invisibly and gradually builds up.

When the Prodigal Son wasn't content, he demanded the father to grant him his own portion of the estate which the father lovingly gave to him. In the times and seasons we are in, it is easy to be pressured to want everything when you feel it is best, but the question is, can you handle what you are asking for? Are you grateful and content with what's in your reach?

It can be discouraging to realise how powerful your gifts are whilst underestimating them. What you don't grow or invest in will be passed on to another person who is more likely to increase the results twice as much. The Prodigal Son experienced a change in his heart. In verse 18, he mentioned that he would go back to his father's house.

When you are able to admit where you have gone wrong, that is the same moment God will come through and show you the way forward. Now, this is a great opportunity to be thankful at all times! The Prodigal Son changed his heart's posture from pride to sorrowful and ultimately grateful that his father didn't abandon him, and that is the same love God has for us where He promises to never leave us where we are.

Abundant Progress

The more thankful I became, the more I started to see my situations change for the better. It is not wise or healthy to wait until your life picks up or you start seeing your plans and desires fall in place, that is when you decide to be thankful. Moments where you will be tested teaches you how to be thankful in the unknown – the seasons where you don't know what tomorrow will hold, but you still choose to remain at peace.

When you think about your life right now, what are the focus points that require you to be thankful, and how does it impact you as an individual? When you are more thankful, your fears and doubts have no power to control you. Being able to remain thankful even when you get feedback that you didn't expect is a level of maturity which takes a shift in the mind. It's the power of a thought that positions you into the heart of gratitude and impacts the way you navigate life.

A reminder for you: When gratitude fills your heart, there is no room for negativity or complaints. Your joy is contagious which draws others to you because the words that come out of your mouth are transferrable. Being grateful starts with an intentional mindset which enables you to reflect back over your life on the great blessings experienced and the ones that are yet to come. Our lives are fleeting and although no-one knows what tomorrow holds, we have today to make it right. Therefore, a heart of gratitude will take you further if you start with embracing the gradual steps.

SIX

'ABUNDANCE' AND 'PROGRESS'

When you combine abundance and progress, they interrelate. The focus point to consider is this: living an abundant life is a step-by-step process that does not happen overnight. Progress is not for the faint-hearted either. Don't be deceived and think that you can short-cut your way to success – it doesn't work that way and shouldn't be considered as an option. You have a responsibility to ensure that your life is making an impact in your respective capacity and this starts with how you see yourself and what you can handle. To add onto this, personal development plays a role towards abundance and progress. Let's break it down further:

- **Personal** = Private
- **Development** = Progress or Construction

As I took the time to present a seminar on building self-confidence and personal development in April 2022, the vision was to enable every attendee to understand what personal development is. Two words came at the time of preparation and they were:

1) Private
2) Construction

The definition of personal development is: *'private progress under construction.'* When you are seeking to become better in certain areas of your life where there is potential to improve, it will take a firm mindset to work on yourself privately before becoming a public inspiration. Anything that is contributed to the betterment of the community must be worked on behind the scenes one step at a time. This is what private progress is about and shouldn't be rushed or prematurely exposed.

Abundant Progress

Development is giving you the opportunity to take the necessary steps on becoming better at what you enjoy doing with the aim of growing. You are going through the construction of building, nurturing and learning new skills whilst enjoying the progress that is being made.

I believe it is God's joy to see His children having a surplus of abundance, but not at the detriment of them becoming attached to temporary pleasures. There is a difference between having an **abundant** life and having a **progressive** life. Let's take a look at the following definitions:

ABUNDANCE – According to the Oxford English Dictionary, the term *abundance* is defined as *"a large quantity that is more than enough."*

PROGRESS – According to the Oxford English Dictionary, the term progress is defined as *"the process of improving or developing, or of getting nearer to achieving or completing something."*

We must learn how to embrace and enjoy progression because it not only keeps us humble, but reminds us that we are still on the journey to discover more about ourselves. In the different stages of life, there will be times where the journey will feel uneasy and sometimes silent, but in those moments, they are teaching you about the beauty of each unique day allowing it to flow organically. No matter how much you desire to achieve, there will always be more that will keep on grabbing your attention, and that is where you must make a decision and ask if it's worth chasing. Your life exists to progressively make an impact to the world and contribute to God's abundance.

What is the difference between the two, however? Abundance is what a person desires; this could be more freedom, more deposable income, excellent health, whilst progress is the steady steps one must take in order to achieve abundance. No matter what you desire, nothing can be enjoyed if you don't cultivate a habit of peace which includes being content with what you have. Two people must make

Abundant Progress

a conscious decision to form a healthy collaboration in order to see growth. If one person is constantly on the receiving end but isn't willing to give what they have, this is a one-sided relationship.

Although there is power in both agreement and disagreement, one's ultimate decision should not affect the other person. The best way to help each other is to communicate and work on solutions together. This is one of the greatest strengths that benefits the other person. It doesn't matter how difficult life's circumstances may be as long as you are willing to be open to change and contribute in ways that add value.

What areas in your life are you intentional about seeing **abundance** in? Tick the most applicable options:

- Health and well-being
- Finances and business
- Family and friends
- Relationships and loved ones
- Community and networking
- Giving and receiving
- Helping the education system
- Other_____

What **progressive** steps are you looking to make to improve your relationship with abundance? Tick the most applicable options:

- Reading more books that will edify the mind, soul and spirit
- Pray with an expectation and concrete plan
- Find other supportive roles to progress in your career
- To not worry and journal every thought on paper
- Enrol on online courses or consider higher education
- Stay away from distractions including social media and negative thinking
- Serve another individual that's in the field you want to get into
- Other_____

Abundant Progress

Prosperity starts in your Spirit before it is manifested in the physical.

When you start thinking about your vision, what thoughts come to mind? Your thoughts gradually become active decisions that starts to manifest; when you believe in what you are writing, you are stretching the mind to believe that it is possible to attain the vision. Discipline is being able to take time out to learn about what the journey is currently teaching you. Remember that you are always changing each day, although you can't see these changes quickly. Learning how to strengthen your spirit before seeing the vision come into fruition takes great strength and resilience. I realise that what manifests in the physical will start in the spirit and being in alignment to God's Will becomes easier for you to accomplish them.

Staying stagnant and remaining where you are for fear of stepping out will not bring the change you desire to see. You need determination, focus, strength and above all; **patience**. The temporal abundant life that is shown on social platforms shouldn't make you question why progress seems slower than usual. *(Refer back to chapter 1 for further expansion)*. If you feel that life is slowing you down, ask yourself where your priorities are.

Dwelling on the past isn't going to help you remain focused. The writer of Ecclesiastes 7:10 says this: *"Do not say 'Why were the old days better than these?' For it is not wise to ask such questions."* Having thoughts of the past may seem better for a while, but it isn't wise and ultimately slows down your progress. No matter what situation you are in, you must keep going to remind yourself that slow progress is better than no progress. Progression and abundance are both gradual. Every slow season is granting you the grace to run the race. Of course, slow growth isn't comfortable, neither is it easy. The expectations of our loved ones wanting to see changes in our lives may cause a lot of pressure, however, we must keep going because we know there is a race to be won.

Abundant Progress

When I resigned from my previous role, the excitement started, but eventually, as I continued pursuing my writing career, I was open to the challenges of what starting a business would entail. I realised that it was the challenges that built my character and confidence in God and the gifts He gave me to initially have the vision. I was recommended a book called *'Faith Driven Entrepreneur'* that speaks about the importance of running a business with the aim to inspire others through the creative skills that God gives us. Reading this book has challenged my perspective on what business is and why God establishes us to be creative entrepreneurs to build His Kingdom.

As I took the time to study Genesis 26:19-22, verse 22 spoke distinctly to me which says: "Isaac moved on from there and dug another well, and no one quarrelled over it. He named it Rehoboth saying 'Now, the Lord has given us room and we will flourish in the land.'" Isaac **refused** to argue with the Herdsmen of Gerar as they demanded that the water Isaac had dug to re-open the wells claimed to be theirs.

Isaac was wise and smart enough to move from the environment and trust God to provide an open door for him to flourish in the land. For this reason, Isaac and his servants were able to enjoy the benefits of abundance because he applied wisdom to his situation. I am sharing this with you because there will be decisions that must be made to increase your impact and influence and mustn't be compromised or being distracted by petty arguments.

If Isaac was to get even with the Herdsmen of Gerar, there would be no opportunity for him to flourish the way God intended. We learn a lot from our ancestors including the mistakes that didn't define them, the strength they received from God to remain focused despite the attacks that came their way, and many other oppositions they faced but still ended up inspiring the present and future generations. You may not have all the resources you need right now, but what you must remember is that **little is big when it's in God's Hands**.

Abundant Progress

Don't doubt what is in your reach because God has already positioned you to receive Heaven's dew and earth's richness – the abundance of grain and new wine is coming your way, so be expectant and work well with what you already have – further study in Genesis 27:28.

In addition to this, Psalm 36:8 speaks about the feast of abundance in our houses, and this is very encouraging for us to hold onto when life becomes difficult. Our homes, our families and those close to us will surely experience great delights of blessings because of the love God has for us. We must not be ignorant of the fact that progression comes with obstacles as well as great triumphs of testimonies and growth. Using the power of words to uproot every problem and renew your mind is vital to fight against every negative thought. Don't give yourself unease when abundance and progress are already following you through God's goodness and mercies.

Maximising the gradual steps of the journey starts with embracing what each season is teaching you and not finding ways to get out of it quickly. When you are exposed to more education, knowledge, wisdom, or networks, you are progressing, but everything that is being taught must be applied throughout your life. Everything you need to have an abundant life starts in the mind. Having an abundant life doesn't mean you have to work tirelessly and forget the importance of rest, however; what is the aim for living an abundant life? Is it to impress others to show them that you are capable of living life independently, or seen a gap in the market that needs to be fulfilled?

When your purpose is greater than who you are, it will cause the right opportunities to locate you. It is easy for anyone to envision abundance in different ways and you may know someone right now with a great upbringing whilst others who haven't had it easy at all. When the situation becomes unbearable, it's easy to give up and lose faith, but in that very moment, God wants to invite you to newness.

Each time I study Isaiah 43:18-19, it makes me more excited about the future: *"Forget the former things; do not dwell on the past. See,*

Abundant Progress

I am doing a new thing! Now it springs up; do you not perceive it? I am making a way in the wilderness and streams in the wasteland."

It takes patience, a deeper understanding and the revelation to grasp what Isaiah is saying because an abundant life starts with leaving the past behind and walking into another chapter of new beginnings. Progress may take a while, particularly when you are experiencing a hard time, however, these moments should make you position yourself to pause and seek God fervently for change in patient expectation. Don't fight the process; work with it allowing it to strengthen you.

Looking at three different men with unique gifts and skills, they were given a bag of talents or (bags of gold) according to their capacities. The first person was given five talents and doubled it to ten. The second person was given two talents and doubled it to four. The third person received one talent and didn't utilise it well and hid it from his master. Focus on Matthew 25:45-47 where it speaks about the wise servants who were in charge of their master's territory to look after the household. It is a blessing when you are granted the opportunity to enjoy your portion of abundance because of 1) tenacity and 2) attitude. In life, you have a choice to utilise what you have and learn how to multiply it.

No matter how small your portion is, see the beauty in it, for it is unwise to compare your progress to another person if you haven't shown yourself faithful in the process. Abundance is about analysing the progressive steps of your gifts and utilising them to the best of your ability. The moment an intentional decision is made, your thoughts, talents and skills will work for you and eventually be evident to all. However, this requires self-discipling and working on the current season you are in, not wanting to be elsewhere but to remain focused on each day.

We seek what tomorrow holds and haven't finished today's season.

Abundant Progress

Abundance and progress work hand-in-hand – they are seeds that take time to grow which requires patience, faith, positivity, words of wisdom and a servitude heart. Abundance and progress teach you about the beauty of small beginnings; getting you to a place that you couldn't reach on your own if you were to rush the process and forfeit the key lessons that were endeavouring to teach you. I enjoy learning from past disappointments because it helps me to know how to avoid them in the future. Freedom, wealth and happiness comes with a cost including giving your time, sacrificing and working on yourself to be better.

The most important gift to have as you continue life is developing an environment of unity. Don't underestimate how far you can go with other people. It's a beautiful gift when God places destiny helpers in your life to keep you going. *Those who were present in your struggle have every right to celebrate your abundance.* On the other hand, when you want to give up because abundance seems long, ask yourself what purpose you had in mind to start with. Was it only to please your own gains? If you work hard at what you do, great abundance will come to you, but merely talking about getting rich while living to only pursue your pleasures brings you face-to-face with poverty in reference to Proverbs 14:23.

We've been given gifts that suit what we are capable of doing and those gifts are what brings abundant progress. Focus on what you are good at and learn to nurture it with time. Write down your weaknesses and be confident that they will turn into strengths. Don't hide your failures; they contribute to your journey of abundance. Respect is given to the transparent and those who are willing to admit they were wrong to start again. Living a life of truth and honesty are key attributes to building a community of people where they can be real with one another.

It's not in our power to always be strong as this is a form of pride, and for this reason, this is why God remains our Solid Rock. It's good to know that we don't have to understand life on our own and releasing every tension of trying to make everything work. No one has a perfect life including those you admire. It takes an expectant heart to believe that what you have been waiting for is already **in**

Abundant Progress

you. Each day, you have a choice to live – God has given us freewill, however, the life you live will always follow you, so remember to ask yourself how you want to be remembered.

Each day brings grace that keeps you going and taking small steps to overcome challenges that will occur. Notice how I didn't say 'may' occur, because each day *will* present their own challenges, whether it is mental, physical, psychological, emotional, spiritual, social etc. However, when you discipline your mind and avoid strife, it will help in contributing to a well-lived life. It is crucial that we **live real** and not hide under the pressure society brings. The community wants to know the real you which builds trust, connections and divine destiny helpers that are able to support you on the journey. They may not follow you through to the end, but there are key lessons that will be learnt from their time spent with you.

Abundance and progress comes with various life lessons and the strength to learn from them without giving up on the journey. It is important to reflect on the type of abundant lifestyle you want to have, whether that is to be financially stable, giving generously to others, improving on your physical, emotional and mental well-being, being present with your children and able to invest in their future education, learning and life skills. Abundance has to reach more people than yourself. Your journey of abundance starts with being able to embrace the progressive stages of your life and look at it with expectation knowing that the best is yet to come.

A reminder for you: Living your life with integrity and a good reputation will be remembered over wealthy possessions as Proverbs 22:1 tells us. When your life is pleasing to the Lord, it will cause breakthroughs to occur. Be mindful to remain humble when progression comes your way; it's good when the results are coming through, but remember where you started to remind you of God's favour on your life. A hint of pride can take you down immediately, so let this be a reminder as you progress along the journey.

Abundant Progress

SEVEN

YOUR FAITH MATTEERS

Where do I start with **faith**? At times, our faith does have challenges, not only to believe in what we can't see, but to stand on the promises that have been spoken over us, knowing that at the appointed time, they will all fall in place. Faith is in stages; your faith can make you think greater thoughts or cause you to shrink and stay in the same position. When it comes to understanding why your faith matters, it is important to consider the following:

- Being surrounded by a community of faith-believers to encourage you on the journey.
- To not cut your faith short when the promise seems long.
- Faith pleases God to move on your behalf nurturing it with positive words and thoughts that contribute to your personal and professional growth.

Faith has been my standing ground in every season of life. When it was easy, I had faith; when it was difficult, I had to *build* my faith through the Word of God, spending time in His Presence (and I don't say this lightly), and remembering the fact that whatever happens, God is still good. What faith teaches me isn't just for my own benefit, but for future generations.

It's easy for anyone to have faith when their plans are going accordingly, but building faith in difficult circumstances will stand the test of time. When you don't know what tomorrow holds and you still have faith to believe that it will be a great day, that's how you grow.

Your faith is stretched further when your desires don't seem to be in alignment. You will understand this as your walk with God increases.

Abundant Progress

Your faith matters when it comes to building gradual abundance, although it will take time. When you have an unfinished job, you realise that it's not about fulfilling the job or making it to the final destination, but utilising the faith when more tasks are given to continue the journey.

Why do we always want our faith to work when it is in our favour? We must get to a stage where our faith is constantly stable and unchanging. Just like our Father who is firm in all of His ways. Because He has faith in you, you must also have faith in Him.

When your faith is being tested, how do you respond? Take the time to write your answer below:

_____

_____

_____

_____

_____

_____

No matter what stage you are in life, there will be moments where your emotions and your faith are battling with each other. When those moments come, don't force to fight it in your own strength; speak and call out your emotions reminding them of your faith.

In order to protect your faith, you will also need to be wise with who you speak to when you are in the building stages. These are the most pivotal moments of your faith journey because how you start and how you finish isn't going to be the same.

Abundant Progress

You learn greater lessons in the middle stages, but how to carry on will depend on the level of your faith.

Think of it this way; you have a friend or family member who you love dearly. One day, they may decide to mistreat you; in this case, will your faith be shaky or will it stand firm? God grants us opportunities to continue trusting Him because of His unchanging nature. We may be in the wrong, yet, His love surpasses our faults. Therefore, your faith can increase because you are aware of your undeserving love from a Mighty God.

In the meantime, keep your faith and keep on waiting, because those who wait the longest enjoy the greatest. There is beauty in the wait because patience is being developed and you will understand that great results isn't produced in a day. Don't rush. God's timing is absolutely gorgeous.

When you are going through certain situations, from experience, you can look back over your life and think about the moments where you cried for a particular prayer to be answered, and when God revealed in a dream or vision as to why God had to stop it, you will lift up your hands and thank Him for what He saved you from. The beauty of prayer is that it initiates change and stirs up a strong focus that can't be distracted because of your determination to see the blessing come to fruition.

I emphasise on the importance of faith-building towards your mental and emotional well-being. Our thoughts are constantly in mental mode from the time we sleep to not having enough time to relax and take each day as it comes. I do believe that rest is one of the key attributes to a productive and fulfilling life. When your body requires you to rest, listen to it.

Proverbs 3:6 tells us to **acknowledge** God in all our ways so that He will direct our paths. The beauty of this scripture is being aware that God exists and His Presence is with us everywhere we go. We know that to acknowledge someone means that we create space and allow them to reign over us.

Abundant Progress

Through every path we encounter, some painful, some silent, some unknown and uncertain moments, we are able to continue to walk in the light. We must admire the people in our lives who contribute to our spiritual growth and well-being within our families and in the community.

When you cherish people, you acknowledge that they are valuable to you. Your faith has a direct impact on your trust in God, and when you can trust His character, belief increases. Even in the silent seasons, faith is working for your good; not everything that is given to you all the time is healthy. You may not be able to handle it or carry the weight of the blessing.

Remember that every gift from above is beautiful, but given at the wrong time can make you misuse it. There will be moments in our lives where we must slow down and take it one step at a time. Externally, you don't have it; internally, your character and patience are being built and transformed, and in God's eyes, you are in the right place at the right time.

To build your faith, you have to accept the season you are in and stop pushing your way through. Everyone's race isn't the same, and what someone can do quickly can be a danger zone if you imitate them. When you feel that your faith is wavering, it isn't the time to speak negativity or blame the devil.

It is the time to look back over your life and count your blessings. The power of building faith is through being thankful because you realise that you didn't get to the position alone. God orchestrated people throughout your journey to speak words of healing and restoration when your faith was being tested.

We must be disciplined to make peace with our seasons and understand what the moments are teaching us.

What kind of restoration are you looking for? Do you want the restoration that can't be traded for anything else? Let's talk about

Abundant Progress

the woman at the well in John 4 – she had a great encounter with Jesus that turned her life around for good. Before meeting with the Lord, people didn't know the value she carried, until she desired more! How deep do you want to be changed? You have to be intentional about it, just like this woman.

Encountering the Lord changed her life for good, and the water she asked for wasn't found in a partner, possessions or fame; it was found in the One that knew her before she was born.

Stepping out in faith to the unknown takes great confidence. What leap of faith did you take to come out of your comfort zone? Write your answers below:

_____

_____

_____

_____

_____

_____

_____

Why does prosperity and abundance start by faith? Because **faith** is what ignites you to receive the blessing or promise in your spirit before it becomes a reality. When something is birthed outside the Will of God, it will not last because the One that has authority over your desires hasn't been informed. This also applies to how you work your faith – when you have faith, it is to prepare you for what is to come.

When you have a desire or a creative idea, you don't just have faith in the idea, you have faith in the God who gave you the desire to be creative.

Abundant Progress

Faith can only take you as far as you want to go, but it must be backed up with action. We can't expect to do nothing and hope that everything will fall in place. Even if you try something new and fail, you will look back and be thankful that you tried. I honour those who endeavour to work on their goals; some that have started businesses and perhaps it didn't work out the way they'd expected it are still inspirational because they made the bold step.

Yes, it may not have been their path or they wanted to try something new, but the key is to make an attempt. We have all tried something throughout our lives that we thought would work. Perhaps you were eager to create an additional service to your existing business but wasn't able to secure any clients. God sees your faith and that in itself is an achievement.

Most times, what we are trying to build may not always be in the Will of God, so we must be very prayerful to know what we need to focus on and what we should avoid so our valuable time isn't being wasted. The more honourable you are to God, the easier it is to hear His voice.

Being humble starts in your mind as well as building your faith muscles. With time, you will realise that as God is lifting you up, it will require much humility and grace to remember where you started from, and acknowledging the gift of faith given to you on the journey.

Nobody has faith to fail; of course not! But through failure, it builds stronger faith.

If you haven't been through the pressures of failure or doubt, you won't know how to appreciate success when it comes. Anyone can smile when everything is working well, but for those who are intentional about abundance, remember it is a faith-process. Don't shortcut your faith because there are key lessons that can only be

Abundant Progress

taught through the fire. Faith is not a plan b alternative. It is your primary source of belief.

What you desire must be confirmed in your spirit because faith can't be seen, but revealed. What you can't see is greater than what you can see, therefore, it is leading you into paths of stretching, pruning and focus.

The test of faith will eventually bring the greatest testimony. When you are inspired by the success of another individual, did you take the time to listen attentively to their story, because so often, we are amazed about their triumphs, but forget that there were thorns and obstacles that one had to climb to overcome.

When you overlook someone's story and assume life has been a smooth ride, you miss a key lesson – the pruning stages of faith and character-development. What you had in mind and what you wanted to achieve are always in battle because it is not in God's Will for you to go ahead of Him. I want you to think attentively about this question – "Are you ready for what you are asking for?" or is it becoming a mere fantasy in your mind that you aren't willing to be disciplined enough and prepare for the responsibilities that come with abundance?

The journey is not for the swift and anything that is going to be costly will take time. God's plan for you doesn't involve worrying as Philippians 4:6 says, but through the uncertainty, we learn to trust Him in all our decisions.

The more it becomes difficult to trust God is the moment you've taken your eyes off Him and focusing on the situation at hand. You will eventually realise that the season He put you through was preparing you for the greater manifestation. However, allowing fear to tamper with your faith forfeits and defeats the purpose of the waiting season.

Cutting corners to get to the promise is the main reason why progress seems slower. Without seeking the One who knows every detail about your life and trusting in your own resources causes your

Abundant Progress

faith to be shattered. Being consistent in communicating with God is one of the greatest and peaceful ways you gain clarity and find purpose.

If you appreciate your journey of faith, it will surely help you to increase your prayer life and slow down from the world's standards of success. There is nothing in the world that you are missing as long as you are in the Will of God.

As you are growing in your walk of faith, you will definitely encounter people that will have doubts with faith. You can set healthy boundaries to ensure that your faith-relationship isn't interrupted by others, yet still being graceful to those who are still building their faith-journey. God has given you His Spirit to stand boldly and speak blessings and abundance into your life through words. Your words are seeds when you nurture them with God's truth! For this reason, I want you to refuse and stop declaring these following phrases starting from today:

- *"I can't buy it – it's too expensive!"*
- *"I can't do this – I don't have enough resources!"*
- *"I don't have it; leave me alone!"*
- *"I can't seem to make ends meet; there is no point."*
  "I am struggling – can't you see how difficult life already is?"

Monitor what is in your environment before you communicate. **Observe** and **listen** first. At some stage in our lives, we've encountered seasons where fear was comfortable and chose not to do anything about it; rather, we made more excuses which created lazier environments to pray less and complain more.

When you speak the right words into your soul, it's remembering how many deposits you've made and this is what should make you accountable for your faith journey. Don't wait until someone has faith before you believe, because your faith isn't dependent on someone's else ability to believe. You have to believe for yourself and let that conviction continue to manifest in your life.

Abundant Progress

At times, it's the fear of trying to believe and feeling like it isn't going to work that stops you from taking that big leap of faith. Have you taken the time to speak to yourself on a one-to-one to reflect on the life you desire to live?

What legacy are you looking to pass down onto your generation because how you live life right now impacts the future generation. It is the struggle that we have all been through in several ways that strengthens us, making it easier for our children and their children to live better lives. As Numbers 6:24-26 talks about the **Priestly Blessing** we ought to be reminded that what we go through is for the benefit of the wider community. They will see our lives and how God has strengthened us through the challenging moments. We must be thankful for the struggles as evidence of God's providence and grace throughout our lives.

Listening to what someone has gone through and how they've managed to encourage themselves and continue the journey is inspiring. People who have less are able to produce more effectively and increase it because of their faith and how intentional they've believed in what they value.

The more you value what you have, the better God is able to bless you with more.

As I was studying about The Parable of the Sower in *Matthew 13:12* what inspired me was in verse 12 which states that 'whoever has will be given more, and they will have an abundance.' – this speaks volumes because it is possible to have plenty and still be given more, however, in the latter part of verse 12, it tells us that what you have can be taken away if not used wisely. This parable focuses not only on the seed that is sown, but the **faith** that's involved in gaining the harvest.

To the one that was able to multiply was due to their diligent faith, work ethic and mindset to believe that they will receive it; to the latter, the individual lost what they already possessed because they

Abundant Progress

were focused on their lack, rather than seeking wisdom and being able to add value to what is already in their reach.

You must get to a stage in your life where no matter what comes your way, you will keep on persevering. You have to be positioned to desire more and envision the abundant life God has promised you. Having this mindset will remind you of the importance of community, fellowship and helping one another. A person who has a heart for others will be fulfilled as Proverbs 11:25 (NIV) says – "A generous person will prosper; whoever refreshes others will be refreshed."

Having this lifestyle and mindset is a choice; stop allowing the way you feel to dictate what you do or don't deserve. It is the faith you have in God that will take you further than where you currently are.

Another key scripture to building your faith is in Luke 1:45 (NIV) and it says "Blessed is she who has believed that the Lord would fulfil His promises to her." This scripture reveals a lot from a wider spectrum, particularly when what's in our reach seems unattainable. The more you are in seasons of doubt is the moment your faith must rise up and take action.

We don't have to wait for our lives to get better before believing that it has already changed. It is not fit to raise a generation where we teach the future leaders that waiting for the perfect opportunity will come when we just expect it and not take **action**. When it comes to your faith, it is attached to God's promises over your life. It takes strength to persevere when life becomes difficult, but having your faith keeps you persistent.

You can still have strong faith for the future and at the same time, keep your focus on the present. Our faith seems to be more on what is yet to come than on what is currently in our reach because of what we can see. At times, you may get frustrated at your life or those around you, but coming across Romans 14:1 it says: "Accept the one whose faith is weak without quarrelling over disputable matters." What an enlightening and encouraging verse.

Abundant Progress

This can positively contribute to ones' progress as it reassures understanding and patience. The working of your faith builds character, and your character builds integrity.

Your integrity is what others are attracted to, and not necessarily the results, and for this reason, it's important to give other people grace when they fail to have strong faith.

There is Grace given when your faith is shaky!

Our walks in life aren't going to be the same which is why it's vital to ensure that we take it easy with those who are surrounded within our community, as we all possess different strengths and weaknesses, notwithstanding the fact that our faith still speaks on our behalf even in difficult situations. Society has made it seem that if you aren't at a specific level at a certain age, what have you achieved – this is instant gratification that doesn't last and will make you work tirelessly to get to a level that didn't exist in the first place.

I believe in working organically to obtain results that are long-lasting and have valuable impact on the lives of others, and this is built by faith. In order for others to see you as honest, they will first of all understand the character and attitude you have towards several situations. In business, your desire to see progress is dependent on how relatable, transparent and honest you are with potential and existing clients. For them to trust in the vision, your faith must be invested in their pain points, not only in what you can get from them. Business is less about yourself and more about your audience, and it will require humble faith to nurture positive relationships and maintain healthy communication as time goes by. You are not only in business to win, but to inspire other people as well.

Your faith will be tested and it will go back and forth, but you have the choice to keep feeding it with words of prophecy and declaration. Your life isn't going to change until you seek the God of abundant change. When your faith is being tampered with, that is the greatest opportunity to worship and praise God. Give your full

Abundant Progress

attention to the One that can handle life's pressures. Through adoration and stillness before Him, your faith becomes stirred and is set free from past attacks.

However, being able to pass the tests of attacks and fear of the unknown is through believing. In Matthew 13:58, it reminds us that where there is no belief, there won't be any miracles. What is stopping you from believing in what is yours? You may not see it with your physical eyes, nonetheless, how you perceive life to be is what will present itself to you.

I am a strong advocate of self-belief and speaking words of affirmation over my life. Once this becomes a consistent routine, the doubts gently fade away. When the struggles of life come knocking at your door, do you open it anxiously or boldly? Getting to the stage of abundance is a lifetime journey and it will take faith to continue. I know when it comes to manifesting more than you believe, doubtful thoughts can come in and this could be due to expectations that are unrealistic or disappointments from the past. Don't allow your thoughts or desires to make you forget the present.

Focus on what is in front of you and make it work accordingly. Every time you feel out of place, rather than working harder, take the time to soak, unwind and relax. Learn to bask in the present and allow yourself to laugh and learn from the mistakes made in the past.

When reflecting over Ephesians 3:20, what comes to mind? The words of abundance, progression, favour, outpouring, progress; you name it. Your faith is what will ignite Ephesians 3:20 (ESV) to come to life. It says: "Now to Him who is able to do far more abundantly than all that we ask or think, according to the power at work within us." At times, we may feel unworthy of asking for more or decide to remain content with 'just enough.' Living a life of abundance is having the confidence to ask for more on the level you are on with the aim of handling your portion wisely.

Asking for more requires greater responsibility, for to whom much is given, much more is required – in reference to Luke 12:48. It is your faith that will keep you grounded in all you've asked for, but

Abundant Progress

being able to believe for impossible blessings is the next level we must learn how to abundantly progress in.

It may take some time to reach that level, especially where we are living in a society where instant gratification is the norm, but something must change within you, starting from the relationship you have with faith. The aim of this book reminds you that faith is a priority. When life becomes more difficult, that is when you must hold onto the anchor of your faith because it is a personal relationship that you have to believing for greater.

Do not give in to fear or worry; those robbers of abundant living!

When worry and fear are present, feed it with faith and optimism, even when your feelings are telling you to forfeit the journey. Don't get comfortable waiting for change to come when you are in the position to take those gradual steps to start the process enabling you to admit where your weaknesses are and be willing to work on them daily with grace and gentleness.

A reminder for you: Be determined to believe in the best for every situation. Doubting doesn't bring the breakthrough. You gain by believing; not being hesitant or worrying. Yes, worry is a natural emotion, however, you must turn it into praise and thanksgiving by writing and speaking words of restoration into every doubtful moment, for Jeremiah 33:6b says that *God will grant His children abundant peace and security*. Hold on to your peace and remain secure to know that your future is beautiful as you develop your faith in Him.

EIGHT

EXCELLENCE TO EXCELLENT

When you are intentional on working with excellence in your environment and the community, it will impact your character and the way you live. Challenges will come, however, when you are able to go through the valleys and dark seasons, it prunes you and sharpens your ability to persevere. The transformation of excellence to excellent is learning from the dips and detours of life.

We are excited when our plans go the way we want it to, and in all honesty, that is our heart's desires; to ensure that our needs and goals are met. Although we know it doesn't always happen that way, it is pride within that seeks to highlight certain moments of our lives and refusing to show vulnerable moments for fear of being judged.

The moment you give power to fear is the moment you are defeated.

Each day, speak life into yourself by declaring that you will be excellent. To be excellent isn't to be perfect. To be excellent is to surpass ordinary standards despite not having all you need. You are not to look down on yourself and complain about what you don't have, or else, it won't allow you to see the benefits of expansion.

It is not your job to advertise yourself to others for them to see your worth. Being excellent will naturally unfold. Don't look at your life and assume that excellence is in the eyes of others. Casting your pearls too early will cause you to underestimate the value of what you carry inside of you.

When you have been given an opportunity to run a project, or receive an email from a reputable organisation requesting for your expertise through a speaking engagement, the first point of action

Abundant Progress

isn't to expose it immediately, but take it to the Lord in prayer and ask for His wisdom on how to conduct yourself and prepare. An excellent spirit is humble enough to know that he or she is undeserving of such an opportunity, and yet is able to work at it effectively.

Giving society the control to dictate when you should post your achievements that hasn't yet been fulfilled will lead to disappointment. The expectations of pleasing others at the expense of your peace is what we must learnt to avoid.

From excellence to excellent is the silent seasons of hard work, sowing and investing. It is privately progressing under construction to wait in great expectation for God to lift you causing opportunities to find you.

Are you relentless? Are you resilient? Are you working on what you have, or are you watching everyone pass you by? Work on what you've been given with a positive mindset and eventually give it space, time and patience to work altogether for your good. The major plan you had to fulfil the vision is still pending, but what mental changes are you putting in place to see a difference with where you are and where you desire to go? Whether you realise it or not, your season IS already changing!

You have to believe in it before the manifestation becomes physical. The mind plays a strong role in what you do and how you behave. Being excellent is a key character trait that God has given those who He entrusts to do His Will. This could be other creative gifts that you are naturally good at doing that adds value into the lives of others.

Having excellence is where you have multiple gifts that's effectively working to benefit a greater purpose to mankind. When you follow or are attracted to certain individuals, you are following them for a reason because of their excellent spirit and how they conduct themselves in pressuring moments. No matter who you are

Abundant Progress

following, you believe in them and that's why they are on your mind. Remember that it was God who gave these individuals the success to get to where they are today.

Now let's talk about you; what is your definition of an *excellent spirit* and being *excellent*?

Excellent spirit:
_____
_____
_____
_____
_____

Being excellent:
_____
_____
_____
_____
_____

When you stop believing in what God invested in you, it begins to lose influence. Patience plays a pivotal part in your life and the way responsibilities are managed. Our lives are constantly looking for ways to keep going in health, relationships, mastering tasks, working on our mental and emotional well-being and many other areas. When you are providing a service for an individual or going into a new business venture, do it with excellence and the willingness to go the extra mile for the individual or company. Do you know that showing up is bringing value to the table? Your existence to serve with a spirit of excellence is embedded in you.

Abundant Progress

Until they see your success, don't expect everyone to support you.

One of the greatest lessons that I am constantly learning on route to destiny and purpose is that not everyone will understand and that's okay. During the process of being pruned by the different seasons of going into the unknown, it is expected for people not to relate to the vision. The aim is not to force or make anyone understand because we are all on a unique journey. Take a look at the following points which will give you insights into why people may not agree with your vision:

- An **insecurity** which is a detrimental mindset preventing support on your vision. When you focus on certain areas in your life that doesn't seem to be working out, it eventually starts affecting the way you see yourself and the attitude that's developed which eventually starts at the root of bitterness making you want to hide from others who are doing well in their respective fields. We should acknowledge that someone else's journey took time to develop and the importance of working on yourself before giving access to self-doubt. Learn to embrace people's progress and it will make your insecurities shrink.

- **Comparing** your journey to another individual is covered in greater depth in chapter 3. Remember that you are unique and your journey will not be the same as others. Looking at what someone else is doing is one of the easiest ways to fall and become small-minded. The abundant life that you require consists of constantly working on yourself because you aren't in battle without anyone else.

- Being **impatient** with the process opens the door to many distractions around you. When you come out of place because you think your purpose is delayed, it will cause you

Abundant Progress

to start again. You know how it felt to keep pushing and having the motivation to carry on, so what stopped you? What made you question yourself and think you aren't worth it? Why would you want to rush a beautiful piece of work that will be valued by many in the near future?

Be happy when your plans fail; God wants to give you the best!

We should be very mindful of the fact that God doesn't bless what hasn't been ordained for His children. Excellence to excellent is about the journey and not just the destination, but the key lessons learnt during the process. The purpose of Abundant Progress is to remind you that making progress is a daily commitment of dealing with obstacles that come your way one step at a time, particularly the ones you did not see coming.

You may know of someone that is able to handle their own circumstances in a mature manner and start thinking that you are the only one dealing with such issues. Until you express to someone you can confide in, you will end up carrying the same mindset-attitude onto others and expecting a different result.

Before you step into the realm of excellence, the question is; **do you believe in being excellent, and if so, what is holding you back?** Believing in what you desire to see will take time; it may be in one day and for others, it could take five years, but I tell you, it tastes much sweeter when the delay turns into abundance because the longer the wait, the greater the testimony.

Pride stops people from being authentic for fear of talking about their struggles. To the world, showing weakness won't get you far, but to God, your weakness enables His great Power to show you what He has in mind for your life rather than chasing every opportunity that comes your way.

Abundant Progress

Instead, we end up numbing the pain by saying 'Everything is so good right now; I am really enjoying!!' – but deep down, you know there are certain areas that you are desperate for a breakthrough. For your own good, be truthful about what you are facing, and don't allow your ego to stop you from breaking free. It's good to cry and let it all out. It's good to understand that those who you admire have their own struggles too. The scars that make people who they are today is what enables them to be successful. When you desire to start a new project or want to work with someone, it starts with building genuine connections, communicating effectively, and handling criticism well, but above all, seeking God in the secret place.

Throughout my writing journey, there has not been a time where I didn't need God to keep me going. There were some tough moments that made me look within myself and asked whether I could continue the journey and remembered two core values:

1) **Departure of loved ones** – grief and loss play a pivotal role when it comes to building excellence because loss should make you understand that it wasn't there to hurt you, but to remind you that strength comes in broken places and to leave a legacy for those who have gone before us.

2) **Legacy** – when your time is up on earth, what will people say about you? Will they say you lived a life with an excellent spirit? How will your reputation be spoken of other than what you own?

Each time I have reflecting moments, I remember these two values which keep me accountable and humble. No matter who you are, we are all going through circumstances that people won't always understand. We must learn how to mind our own affairs if we aren't going to add value and make a change in the lives of others. From excellence to excellent is about the key lessons of patience, pruning and discipline towards our own lives and what we choose to focus on for the betterment of the future. Questions we have are often repeated silently or outspoken including:

1) When is it *my* turn?

Abundant Progress

2) When am *I* going to see my harvest?
3) When will *I* be able to testify?

There's an eagerness to see every desire fall accordingly in our lives, and it's about how you tune your mind with the way you see life's circumstances that causes your perspective to change. Even in rejection, you learn how to cultivate excellence and do better, because once you are exposed to greatness, the excellence within you will start to flourish.

It can't settle or go back to the way it was. In this case, you learn to be more patient, forgiving and transformed until your mind is renewed because the changes you want to see must first start within you.

I don't believe in fast growth; I believe in gradual growth.

If we don't apply discipline with the decisions made, we get tempted to look at what other people are doing; this can be for the purpose of inspiration, ideas or even encouragement. It's not wrong to watch what others are doing, but the motive and perspective that it's looked from will determine whether you are going up another level or attracting stagnation and complacency.

As I was studying two key proverbs which I will share shortly, I want you to think about a time in your life where you were intentional about multiplying your finances. You were willing to do anything and everything to gain more because you weren't content with the amount you once had.

How did you react and what steps did you take to increase your finances? Write them below:

_____

_____

Abundant Progress

_____
_____
_____
_____
_____

Referring to the two key proverbs, they are:

1) **Proverbs 13:11 (Amplified Version)** says: *"Wealth obtained by fraud dwindles, but he who gathers gradually by [honest] labour will increase [his riches]."*

2) **Proverbs 20:21 (Christian Standard Bible)** says: *"An inheritance gained prematurely will not be blessed ultimately."*

When you think about excellence, how do you believe it is achieved? Tick the option most suited to you:

Option A) In haste
Option B) At a steady pace
Option C) A combination of both
Option D) By utilising what is already in my hands and making it work
Option E) An additional source of income i.e., turning your passion into a business

When completing your tasks with ease, you are more likely to achieve greater in the long term. I tell you this; anything that is done with the right balance and motive will succeed. You are not too slow or too quick to step into your greatness. Each day reveals new lessons, so don't take matters into your own hands. Now, let's ponder on Proverbs 13:11 – wealth gained **hastily** will diminish. The term *hastily* is known for *a hurried individual that is eager to*

Abundant Progress

see excessive results within a short space of time. An example of this could be:

"I am ready to start a business and determined to make a large sum of money", but how is your current cashflow looking at this time? What online courses, workshops, webinars and seminars are you attending that will sharpen your skillset in business? Ultimately, how grateful are you for the season you're in at this time? This is how you will be able to identify whether the business will stand firm. However, it is beautiful and pleasing to know that whoever gathers little by little will increase what they already have. This is to help you understand the importance of small beginnings.

Great abundance doesn't come in haste. You need to take the time to understand why you are getting into a project before considering it. There are many people who are frustrated and tired because firstly, they haven't applied Matthew 6:33 into their decisions which therefore results to what they did not expect to happen. Secondly, when considering the eagerness to move in haste, you must analyse your motives; are they self-centred or trying to prove a point to others?

Does what you desire have the wider community in mind and the authenticity to serve the masses? Is what you are building bigger than yourself? If you are willing to wait with expectation and not get out of alignment but stay in your lane, you will understand that little steps bring long-term results that last and are guaranteed to provoke future generations to live better. Habakkuk 2:3 reminds us that at the appointed time, the vision will come to pass. God honours integrity. Be integral in your decisions and refuse to allow others to dictate where you need to be.

It's not when you reach the level of success that makes life beautiful; it's the stages where God hides and makes you humble enough to serve those who are higher than you.

Anything that doesn't cost you will not last long. The sacrifice to give especially in a difficult season can be very testing, but when

Abundant Progress

done with the right attitude, it will produce abundance because Luke 6:38 encourages us to give generously so that good measure will be pressed down and multiplied back onto us. In addition to this, your life becomes beautiful when you serve those who are higher than you whilst still believing for a breakthrough.

I remember towards the end of December 2021 whilst studying Revelation 22, the key verse that stood out to me was verse 2 which reads: "Down the middle of the great street of the city. On each side of the river stood the tree of life, bearing twelve crops of fruit *yielding its fruit every month* and the leaves of the tree are for the healing of the nations."

You must endeavour to have a fruitful life where you can show something each month of God's faithfulness and His strength carrying you through. My life must produce abundant fruit to not only benefit the community, but the future generations coming after me.

Devaluing what God has placed in you to reach another person's achievements is detrimental to yourself and those around you because you'll end up constantly being on the lookout for every change one decides to make. When you copy other people's ideas, it entertains subtle insecurity to not believe in what you have within. Yes, this is painful, but we must understand that abundant progress is an individual journey. It is not for you to imitate others, but to embrace and appreciate the journey that you are on.

Let's talk about instant gratification and the pressure to increase followers on social platforms. We are living in a world where numbers are constantly increasing, inflation rising and prices going up. We don't honour the process enough for us to stay in the seasons we are in. Instead, we itch, we groan, we moan and complain until our will is done, not knowing that it causes internal destruction.

Most people that are often looked down on are those that have great potential, but their mistake is depending on others too much without being confident in who they are. Instead, they seek a higher approval from those they feel are better than them, which eventually leads to

Abundant Progress

idolism, procrastination and laziness. God is in the business of using people that are underestimated because He knows that their vulnerabilities are the starting point of greatness to show forth His Glory.

Abundance doesn't just start when the numbers increase; abundance starts in your mind before it becomes a reality. You must learn how to embrace failure because no matter what stage you are in, it will come. Don't suppress your troubles, rather, let them build and make you wiser.

Not everyone will give you the luxury of knowing what they are facing. Just listen to the way they speak and that will give you an indication, for out of the abundance of the heart, the mouth speaks. Our speech can strengthen or weaken us; be very careful who you confide in especially when God is pruning and sharpening you in the dark moments.

My Abundance and your emptiness are a perfect match for Me to show you what I can do – God.

There will be moments in your life where coming empty is all God wants. Just come as you are and take off the burdens that have been held on to you. We are all endeavouring to find answers, especially the ones that will solve quick problems, but during the journey of being excellent, it will take time to unfold. When you come with an agenda, your expectations are always to meet them.

However, when God comes with His expectations, are you willing to put yours aside for a greater result? Have you fully surrendered all to Him and not have another back up plan? You may not have much resources right now, but it doesn't mean you should overlook what you already have. Most of the greatest blessings are birthed with what's in your reach rather than trying to look elsewhere for it.

When have you disciplined yourself to be still? Why the restlessness and force in obtaining what already has your name on

Abundant Progress

it? Excellence is already in you whether you realise it or not because those who obey and walk with God will not need to fear anything.

Fear can only have so much power that you give it, and although it comes up from time to time, you have every right in you to shake it off and continue to walk in excellence. Having to work overtime will require a certain level of excellence, patience and the ability to rest well, but when you know your God and put Him in His rightful place, He will allocate the resources, the tools, the time invested and the right divine connections to support you on the journey.

You will understand the importance of unity as you continue building because anything that's bigger than you will require reliable and integral people.

In order to attract excellence, you need to be an excellent individual by how you position yourself. How you can do this will require the following points:

- **How you talk to yourself** – out of the abundance of the heart; the mouth speaks. Your words are sharper than fire. Be intentional about what you say to yourself in seasons of temporal testing.

- **How to position yourself** – if you are not putting in the work, how can others identify who you are or the gifts you have? Being positioned at the right place and at the right time causes the right opportunities to find you.

- **How you think of yourself** – your mind should always be fed with positive thoughts because what starts within will eventually be revealed outwardly. Focus on renewing your mind according to what you desire to see and you will understand that thoughts take you further than works.

- **How much quality time you spend with yourself** – when was the last time you turned off everything? – your phone, social media, socialising, networking, and just spent it alone? *Solitude* is critical especially in seasons of building and birthing silently. Do not allow yourself to be distracted by things around you. Keep focused and enjoy your own company.

- **How much time you put in reading and feeding your mind with wisdom** – it's not only about how many books you read, but the content taken away from each book, digesting it and applying them into your life. It is not wise to buy books and not remember what you learnt from them. Start with one book at a time, journal your thoughts and build wisdom through studying them. Books are valuable tools that increase your mental and emotional strength.

- **How intentional you are to move away from distractions** – distractions don't only come from the external, but also how you define yourself internally. Your doubts and self-limiting beliefs are the greatest barriers stopping you from reaching your destiny. Remove the inner distractions before they keep growing. Assumptions and harsh criticism aren't healthy for you, neither for your environment.

- **Your discipline matters** – What is discipline if it is not utilised wisely? How deep do you want to see your goals reached, or even exceed your expectations? What you discipline shows in your conduct, speech and actions, so ensure you are surrounded by those who are disciplined and put in the work. Leave the outcome to God!

All these attributes add up to abundant progress and can be done one step at a time. Your craft is mastered in stages which produces an excellent spirit. It takes a lot of strength to work on what your gifts are and still endeavour to make abundant choices about the life you want. Mistakes and choices will be made as they are inevitable, but when change happens, you must see it for the betterment of your own good.

Abundant Progress

Be intentional about stepping out of your comfort zone, because there is so much you can learn when you aren't in your normal environment. Staying in the same position and making the same repeated choices doesn't bring about an excellent spirit. Instead, you must understand that **this is your season of growth** – which is a great responsibility to transform the way you think with each passing day.

Whatever you do in life, cultivate an excellent spirit. Doing this without compromising will cause more grace, favour and opportunities to find you. This is why Psalm 92:12 speaks profoundly about those who flourish with a righteous heart will prosper like the palm trees and be fruitful. Being able to multiply and expand what you have is the beauty of transitioning from excellence to excellent. With the right pace and at the appointed time, you are able to identify what you have been called to do and work at it diligently, handling any setbacks that try to distract you. You are able to get yourself back on track because you were exposed to better and now must do better!

A reminder for you: Building on your purpose takes time, and although it may not always be a straightforward path, there is beauty in learning from wrong paths to making it right with God. Being excellent comes with learning from the past and adding value in the lives of others, yet working on yourself each day. Make your life an excellent one so others can be inspired and transformed by the excellence God has placed inside of you.

REFLECTION

Look at life from a different perspective and not only from what you can gain or how many accolades you've achieved. Each day is given to you as a gift to cherish, learn and develop on yourself to be better than you was yesterday. Where there is gradual progress, there is gradual abundance. What have you gained from taking the time to study Abundant Progress? I want to share seven reflective points for you to ponder on before we come to an end:

Reflection 1: Slow growth shouldn't always be seen as a negative trait. You must learn how to see life from a positive perspective and not allow it to lead you into clouded vision. In turn, celebrate others without it affecting who you are as it eventually produces unexpected breakthroughs on your end. There is more than enough for everyone to succeed. Selah.

Reflection 2: When breakthroughs happen, it positions you to be grateful with opportunities of giving thanks. You are able to distinguish abundance when it happens and the moments of progress that build your character and attitude towards life's circumstances. In turn, your faith is constantly being stretched, pruned and worked on by increasing the tenacity within you whilst working with a spirit of excellence.

Reflection 3: Take your life one step at a time because what you can't see now will manifest in due course. Be patient with your own journey even though you can't see your way clear right now. It doesn't necessarily mean you are in the wrong environment. You can grow even when it feels uncomfortable. You are one step away from a permanent change in your life. You will make it; never settle and don't give up on the journey because what duration is teaching you will support your future. Every opportunity to learn in the middle stages requires you to keep looking ahead. You have what it takes to make the most of every season in your life.

Abundant Progress

Reflection 4: Be wise about your thoughts and selective on what you listen to. Abundance is positioning and expecting to grab every opportunity with two hands. Don't cut yourself short or shrink because of what didn't happen. What is rejected today will be the pillar of strength tomorrow.

Reflection 5: Someone is looking up to you to keep going and God entrusts you to continue shining the light for others to see. You have everything in you to live and bask in the abundant life that God has promised you.

Reflection 6: Your vision and purpose aren't over because you are still here. Keep feeding the vision; keep investing in your purpose until multiple ideas and creative gifts are birthed to inspire your generation, for many will be enthused by your story and what you've been through and still, you continue to rise! Your abundant progress starts today by making every moment count.

Reflection 7: Ponder on Deuteronomy 28:11-12: "The Lord will grant you abundant prosperity in the fruit of your womb, the young of your livestock and the crops of your ground in the land He swore to your ancestors to give you. The Lord will open the heavens, the storehouse of His bounty, to send rain on your land in season and to bless all the work of your hands. You will lend to many nations but will borrow from none." This is His promise to you, for God is unlimited in wealth and resources as He owns everything in the world and its fullness thereof in reference to Psalm 24:1. Abundant progress is available to you – embrace it today!

OTHER BOOKS WRITTEN BY ESTHER JACOB

It's Time to Heal – *A woman's journey to self-discovery and freedom.*

Completion – *From the perspective of brokenness.*

From Glory to Glory – *Great beauty in seasons of pain; Strong at the broken places.*

The Power of a Forward-Thinking Mindset – *Breaking strongholds in the mind.*

Confident Face – *Embracing your authentic beauty.*

Abundant Progress – *Maximising the gradual steps of the journey.*

All our books can be found on the Authentic Worth website at
www.authenticworth.com/books

Notes

Notes

Notes

www.ingramcontent.com/pod-product-compliance
Lightning Source LLC
Chambersburg PA
CBHW022043160426
43209CB00002B/55